A Grammar of Anaphora

Linguistic Inquiry Monographs
Samuel Jay Keyser, general editor

A Grammar of
Anaphora

Joseph Aoun

The MIT Press
Cambridge, Massachusetts
London, England

This book was set in VIP Times by Village Typographers, Inc., and printed and bound by Halliday Lithograph in the United States of America.

Library of Congress Cataloging in Publication Data

Aoun, Joseph.
  A grammar of anaphora.

  (Linguistic inquiry monographs ; 11)
  Bibliography: p.
  Includes index.
  1. Anaphora (Linguistics). 2. Generative grammar.
I. Title. II. Series.
P299.A5A68 1985   415   84-26085
ISBN 0-262-01075-5 (hard)
        0-262-51033-2 (paper)

Contents

Series Foreword

We are pleased to present this monograph as the eleventh in the series *Linguistic Inquiry Monographs*. These monographs will present new and original research beyond the scope of the article, and we hope they will benefit our field by bringing to it perspectives that will stimulate further research and insight.

Originally published in limited edition, the *Linguistic Inquiry Monograph* series is now available on a much wider scale. This change is due to the great interest engendered by the series and the needs of a growing readership. The editors wish to thank the readers for their support and welcome suggestions about future directions the series might take.

Samuel Jay Keyser
for the Editorial Board

Acknowledgments

Part of the material presented here is based on my Doctoral dissertation, which was done at the Department of Linguistics and Philosophy at the Massachusetts Institute of Technology. I wish to thank my thesis advisor, Noam Chomsky, and the members of my committee, Ken Hale and Morris Halle. I also wish to thank my friends Adriana Belletti, Hagit Borer, Mike Brody, Jim Higginbotham, Norbert Hornstein, James Huang, Richard Kayne, Jay Keyser, Howard Lasnik, David Lightfoot, Jean Lowenstamm, Jean-Claude Milner, Luigi Rizzi, Tom Roeper, Alain Rouveret, Henk van Riemsdijk, Ken Safir, Barry Schein, Dominique Sportiche, Timothy Stowell, Jean-Roger Vergnaud, Amy Weinberg, and Edwin Williams. Thanks also to my friends and colleagues at the University of Southern California: Bernard Comrie, Edward Finegan, Larry Hyman, Osvaldo Jaeggli, Steve Krashen, Elinor Ocks, and David Pesetsky. Special thanks to Zeina el-Imad and to Anne Mark for her help.

A Grammar of Anaphora

Introduction

Nominal expressions may be divided into three basic categories:

(1)
a. anaphors such as reciprocals and reflexives
b. pronominals such as *he, she*
c. referential expressions; that is, names such as *John*

In the Government-Binding framework outlined in Chomsky 1981, it is assumed that these nominal expressions may be overt, like the examples used in (1), or nonovert. A nonovert anaphor is the empty element coindexed with an NP, namely, NP-trace. A nonovert pronominal element is for instance pro, the phonetically unrealized counterpart of a pronoun. A nonovert referential expression is the empty element coindexed with a *wh*-element, namely, *wh*-trace or variable.

For each type of nominal expression, a binding requirement specifies the domain in which a nominal expression may or may not have an antecedent. These binding requirements are referred to as the *binding principles* or the *binding theory*. Informally speaking, they require *anaphors* to be bound (i.e., to have a c-commanding antecedent) in a certain opaque domain. This opaque domain is the minimal clause (S) or noun phrase (NP) containing the anaphor and a subject or an agreement marker, which in English happens to occur in tensed clauses only. This opaque domain subsumes the familiar Specified Subject Condition and Tensed-S Condition discussed in Chomsky 1973, 1977. As an example, consider the following sentences:

(2)
a. they$_i$ saw each other$_i$
b. *they$_i$ want Peter to see each other$_i$
c. *they$_i$ said that each other$_i$ left

In (2a) no binding requirement is violated. In (2b) and (2c), on the other hand, the binding requirement for anaphors is not satisfied. The reciprocals are not bound in their opaque domain: in (2b) the opaque domain is the embedded clause, which contains a subject; in (2c) it is the embedded tensed clause.

For *pronouns,* the opposite holds: the binding principles require them to be free (not to have a c-commanding antecedent) in the opaque domain:

(3)
a. *they$_i$ saw them$_i$
b. they$_i$ want Peter to see them$_i$
c. they$_i$ said that they$_i$ left

In (3a) the pronominal direct object is bound in its opaque domain, thus violating the binding requirement. In (3b) and (3c), however, no binding requirement is violated since the pronominals are free in their opaque domain—namely, the embedded clause.

Finally, the binding theory requires *referential expressions* not to have a c-commanding antecedent at all:

(4)
a. *he$_i$ said that Mary saw John$_i$
b. *who$_i$ did he$_i$ say that Mary saw x_i

The name *John* in (4a) and the variable x in (4b) are bound by the pronominal subject of the matrix clause *he.* The binding requirement is thus violated: *he* cannot be construed as coreferential with *John* or the variable in (4a–b).

Furthermore, a subset of these nominal expressions is constrained by the *Empty Category Principle* (ECP), which requires NP-traces and variables to be properly governed. Roughly, these nonovert elements are properly governed if they have a local antecedent or if they appear as the complement of a lexical category such as N, V, or P:

(5)
a. *John$_i$ is probable [$_\bar{S}$[$_S$ t_i to leave]]
b. John$_i$ was killed t_i

In (5a) the empty element (NP-trace) is not properly governed; in (5b) it is properly governed by the predicate. As for variables, consider these examples:

(6)

a.   who$_i$ do you think [$_{\bar{s}}$ t_i that [$_S$ John saw x_i]]
b.   who$_i$ do you think [$_{\bar{s}}$ t_i [$_S$ x_i left]]
c.   *who$_i$ do you think [$_{\bar{s}}$ t_i that [$_S$ x_i left]]

Each of these sentences contains an intermediate trace in COMP that is required by the *Subjacency Principle*. This principle—a bounding principle—prevents an element from being moved across more than one bounding node. Since, in English, S at least is a bounding node, the *wh*-element *who* must move first to the embedded COMP, then to the matrix COMP. As usual, each movement will leave a trace. (See Chomsky 1977b for an extensive discussion of the Subjacency Principle.)

The presence of a complementizer such as *that* with a trace in a given COMP is assumed to prevent this trace from acting as a local antecedent for any element in the sentence containing that COMP. In (6a) and (6c) the intermediate trace in COMP fails to act as a local antecedent for the variable. (6c) will violate the ECP since the variable is not properly governed: it is not a complement of a lexical category and does not have a local antecedent. In (6a), however, the variable—although lacking a local antecedent—is properly governed: it is the complement of a lexical category, namely, the embedded predicate. Finally, in (6b) the variable is not a complement of a lexical category but has a local antecedent, namely, the intermediate trace in COMP. In section 2.7.1, we will return to the *[that-t]* effect in more detail.

It is important to note that for variables, the local antecedent relevant to the ECP is different from the one relevant to the binding principles. For the former, the relevant antecedent is in a nonargument position ($\bar{A}$-position); for the latter, it is in an argument position (A-position). An A-position is a position that receives a grammatical function. According to this characterization, COMP position is an $\bar{A}$-position. With respect to the binding theory, the variable must be A-free (it must not have an antecedent in A-position), and with respect to the ECP, it may be $\bar{A}$-bound (it may have an antecedent in $\bar{A}$-position). In (6b), for instance, the variable is $\bar{A}$-bound by the intermediate trace in COMP.

More generally, the binding theory is a theory of A-binding: it refers solely to antecedents that are in A-positions. An anaphor must be A-bound in the opaque domain determined by the binding principles, a pronominal must be A-free in this opaque domain, and a referential expression must be A-free. As an example, consider the anaphors in (7a–b):

(7)

a.   John$_i$ hates himself$_i$

b.   *which man$_i$ does himself$_i$ hate x_i

In (7a) the anaphoric relation between the reflexive *himself* and *John* is licit, since the antecedent is in an A-position. In (7b) the anaphoric relation between the reflexive and *which man* is illicit, since the *wh*-element is in an $\bar{A}$-position.

We have seen that the distribution of various nominal expressions may be accounted for through the interaction of three sets of principles: the binding theory, the Subjacency Principle, and the Empty Category Principle. The binding theory, a theory of A-binding, is concerned with the relations of anaphors, pronouns, names, and variables to potential A-antecedents. The Subjacency Principle is part of the bounding theory that imposes locality conditions on antecedent-trace relations but not on other antecedent-anaphor relations such as the one that exists between an overt anaphor and the element it is related to. The ECP, which is part of the theory of government, constrains traces only— NP-traces and *wh*-traces—but not other nonovert elements such as pro:

(8)

a.   Binding theory: a theory of A-binding

b.   Bounding theory: Subjacency Principle

c.   Government theory: Empty Category Principle

In linguistic studies conducted in the framework of generative grammar, the theory of government and the theory of binding play a fundamental role; hence the characterization of the framework I am assuming as the *Government-Binding* theory. In this book I will suggest the elimination of some principles and the reformulation of others that form the core of this theory.

An anaphoric relation holds between an anaphoric expression and an antecedent in an A-position. I will demonstrate the existence of another kind of anaphoric relation: one that holds between an anaphor and an antecedent in an $\bar{A}$-position. I will refer to anaphors that need an antecedent in an A-position as *A-anaphors* and to anaphors that need an antecedent in an $\bar{A}$-position as *$\bar{A}$-anaphors;* moreover, I will show that for each type of A-anaphor, there exists a corresponding $\bar{A}$-anaphor. Two symmetric anaphoric systems will thus be distinguished: the A-anaphoric system, whose members are A-anaphors, and the $\bar{A}$-anaphoric system, whose members are Ā-anaphors. To establish the existence of these two anaphoric systems, to study their behavior, and to explore the consequences of their incorporation in the grammar will be my chief concern in this book. Specifically, the distribution of Ā-anaphors, like the distribution of A-anaphors, will appear to be constrained by the binding theory. This theory will therefore have to be generalized from a theory of A-binding—that is, from a theory constraining A-anaphors—to a theory of A- and Ā-binding. The generalized binding theory will be shown to apply in both the Syntax and the Logical Form components of the grammar. Consequently, it will be possible to dispense with the ECP and to derive its effects from the theory of binding and the theory of thematic roles (the theory concerned with the assignment of thematic roles such as agent-of-action, object-of-action, etc.—henceforth, θ-roles). These modifications will be shown to solve various empirical and conceptual inadequacies in the grammatical theory.

The book is divided into five chapters. Chapter 1 examines the behavior of reciprocal constructions in Italian. It will appear that in order to account correctly for the distribution of reciprocal elements in this language, the notion of Ā-anaphoric relation must be incorporated in the grammar. A-anaphors may be overt or not and may bear an independent θ-role or not. This characterization gives four types of A-anaphor and, if applied to the Ā-anaphoric system, four corresponding types of Ā-anaphor. Chapter 2 is concerned with the first type of Ā-anaphor; we will see there that variables are characterized as nonovert Ā-anaphors bearing an independent θ-role. This type of Ā-anaphor, subject to the generalized binding theory, must be A-free and Ā-bound in its governing category. Given the assumption that variables are Ā-anaphors, the role that the ECP plays with respect to these elements will be derived from the binding requirements. For NP-traces, the role of the ECP will be derived from the θ-theory. Its effects being obtained from other sources, the ECP—hitherto responsible for various inadequacies—will be dispensed with.

Chapter 3 has two main themes: the application of the generalized binding theory and the characterization of the notions "anaphor," "pronoun," and "nonovert category." Through the study of processes applying in Logical Form, the binding theory will be shown to apply at the output of each component where anaphoric relations are checked—that is, at the output of Syntax and of Logical Form. Anaphors (I will suggest) lack a complete matrix; hence the need for an antecedent to identify them. With respect to empty elements, I will argue that there is no type distinction between phonetically realized pronouns and the so-called nonovert categories—NP-traces, *wh*-traces, PROs, and pros.

Chapter 4 deals with a second type of $\bar{A}$-anaphor. This is the nonovert $\bar{A}$-anaphor that lacks an independent θ-role: the gap coindexed with the clitic. The distribution of this element in the causative constructions of French will require reformulating the opaque domain in which the binding requirements apply in terms of chains: the notions "accessible chain," "thematic chain," and "argument structure" will be introduced.

Chapter 5 investigates the relevance of $\bar{A}$-anaphora and generalized binding in the study of negation and quantification. Negative constructions in Romance instantiate the third type of $\bar{A}$-anaphor: the overt $\bar{A}$-anaphor that has an independent θ-role. The scope properties of quantifiers will be characterized in terms of the generalized binding theory. Finally, the fourth type of $\bar{A}$-anaphor—the overt $\bar{A}$-anaphor that has no independent θ-role—will be illustrated in existential constructions.

Chapter 1
A Symmetric Theory of Anaphora

In this chapter I will illustrate the empirical necessity of the notion "$\bar{\text{A}}$-anaphor": in order to account for the distribution of reciprocals in Italian, this notion must be incorporated in the grammar. After establishing the existence of $\bar{\text{A}}$-anaphors, I will turn to some of their properties.

1.1 Reciprocals in Italian

The reciprocal in Italian is expressed either by the clitic form *si*, homophonous with the reflexive clitic, or by the discontinuous expression *l'uno . . . l'altro* 'the one . . . the other'. We will be concerned with the latter case. (The discussion of the Italian constructions is based on Belletti 1982, although the analysis that I will suggest differs in various respects from Belletti's.)

The two members of the discontinuous reciprocal expression must be separated by a preposition, as in (1), or by an NP, as in (2):

(1)
a. i miei amici   parlano l'uno dell'altro
    my   friends speak   one   of the other
    'my friends speak of each other'

b. *i miei amici   parlano dell'un(o) l'altro
    my   friends speak   of one   the other

(2)
a. hanno criticato l'uno le idee   dell'altro
    (they) criticized one   the ideas of the other
    'they criticized each other's ideas'

b. *hanno criticato le idee   dell'un(o) l'altro
    (they) criticized the ideas of each other

The members of the reciprocal expression seem to enter into a binding relation:

(3)
a. quei reporters ammiravano l'uno [$_{NP}$ le foto   dell'altro]
     those reporters admired   one   the pictures of the other
     'those reporters admired each other's pictures'
b. *quei reporters ammiravano l'uno [$_{NP}$ le tue foto   dell'altro]
     those reporters admired   one   your pictures of the other

The contrast between (3a) and (3b) illustrates a standard Specified Subject Condition effect. In (3b) the association between *l'uno* and *l'altro* is blocked by the subject of the NP in which *l'altro* occurs.

    The reciprocal expression as a whole (or alternatively *l'uno;* see below) must be related to an antecedent in an A-position, as shown in (4), which is the standard paradigm illustrating the behavior of anaphors:

(4)
a. i miei amici hanno parlato l'uno dell'altro per tre giorni
     'my friends spoke about each other for three days'
b. *Mario ha parlato l'uno dell'altro
     'Mario spoke about each other'
c. Mario ha sostenuto che i miei amici parlarono l'uno dell'altro
     'Mario maintained that my friends spoke about each other'
d. *i miei amici sostennero che Mario parlò l'uno dell'altro
     'my friends maintained that Mario spoke about each other'
e. *i miei amici mi hanno costretto a parlare l'uno dell'altro
     'my friends obliged me to speak about each other'
f. ho costretto i miei amici a parlare l'uno dell'altro
     'I obliged my friends to speak about each other'

The ungrammaticality of sentences (4b), (4d), and (4e) is straightforwardly accounted for by the binding theory. In all these sentences, the reciprocal expression does not have an antecedent in the opaque domain (governing category) in which it occurs. In (4b) the reciprocal does not have an antecedent. In (4d) and (4e) the reciprocal does not have an antecedent in its governing category, which is the embedded clause. On the other hand, (4a), (4c), and (4f) contain no binding theory violations and are therefore grammatical.

    In brief, two anaphoric relations are at work in the reciprocal constructions of Italian:

(R1): the anaphoric relation between *l'uno* and *l'altro*
(R2): the anaphoric relation between *l'uno* and an A-antecedent

Alternatively, (R2) may be formulated as the anaphoric relation between *l'uno* . . . *l'altro* as a whole and an antecedent.

I will now argue that (R1) is an instance of an $\overline{A}$-anaphoric relation. That is, for (R1) *l'uno* (the antecedent of *l'altro*) is in an $\overline{A}$-position, and for (R2) the antecedent of *l'uno* is in an A-position:

(R1) is an $\overline{A}$-anaphoric relation: *l'uno* is the $\overline{A}$-antecedent of *l'altro*.
(R2) is an A-anaphoric relation: *l'uno* needs to be related to an A-antecedent.

The fact that (R2) is an A-anaphoric relation is obvious: in (4a), (4c), and (4f) the antecedent of *l'uno* is in a subject position (A-position). In order to establish that (R2) is an $\overline{A}$-anaphoric relation, we must show that *l'uno* (the antecedent of *l'altro*) is in an $\overline{A}$-position. In this respect, note that when *l'uno* is in an A-position, the association between *l'uno* and *l'altro* is no longer constrained by the binding theory. This is shown by (5), which directly contrasts with (3b):

(5)
l'uno ammira le tue foto dell'altro
'one admires your pictures of the other'

In (5) *l'uno* is in an A-position—a subject position. The association between *l'uno* and *l'altro* is not blocked by the subject of the NP in which *l'altro* occurs. In short, when *l'uno* is in an $\overline{A}$-position, as in (3b), the association between *l'uno* and *l'altro* is subject to the Specified Subject Condition—the binding theory. However, when *l'uno* is in an A-position, the association between *l'uno* and *l'altro* is not subject to the binding theory. Sentences such as (5) also indicate that not only the anaphoric relation (R1) but also the anaphoric relation (R2) ceases to exist when *l'uno* is in an A-position. Neither (5) nor (6) contains an antecedent for *l'uno:*

(6)
confondo sempre l'uno con l'altro
'I always confuse one with the other'

Since (R1)—and for that matter (R2)—exists when *l'uno* is in an $\overline{A}$-position and since for (R1) *l'uno* is the antecedent of *l'altro*, (R1) is an instance of an $\overline{A}$-anaphoric relation: *l'uno* is the $\overline{A}$-antecedent of *l'altro*.

1.2 Symmetric Anaphoric Systems

Having established the existence of $\overline{\text{A}}$-anaphoric relations, let us now investigate some of their general properties. Note first that the binding theory as formulated in Chomsky 1981 (henceforth, LGB) is a theory of A-binding; it is solely concerned with A-anaphoric relations. From our discussion of reciprocal constructions in Italian, it appears that this theory must be generalized to constrain both A- and $\overline{\text{A}}$-anaphoric relations.

In the Government-Binding (GB) theory, A-anaphoric expressions may be overt or not: the reflexive in (7a) is an overt anaphoric expression, whereas the empty category in (7b) left by the extraction of a noun phrase—NP-trace—is not:

(7)
a. John$_i$ hit himself$_i$
b. John$_i$ was hit t_i

The anaphoric expression may also receive an independent thematic role (θ-role) or not. That is, it may or may not have an interpretation different from the one its antecedent has. In (7a) the reflexive anaphor is interpreted as the patient y that was hit by $x,$ and *John* is interpreted as the agent x that hit $y.$ In this case it happens that $x = y.$ In (7b) the anaphoric trace does not seem to receive an interpretation distinct from that of its antecedent *John.* Since A-anaphoric expressions may be overt or not and since they may bear an independent θ-role or not, they may be classified as follows with respect to the features [$\pm\theta$-role], [$\pm$overt]:

(8)
a. [$+\theta$-role, $+$overt]
b. [$-\theta$-role, $+$overt]
c. [$-\theta$-role, $-$overt]
d. [$+\theta$-role, $-$overt]

GB theory acknowledges the natural-language occurrence of three of the four possibilities. Case (8a) is instantiated by reciprocals and reflexives, and case (8c) by NP-traces; see the preceding discussion of (7a–b). Case (8d) is instantiated by pronominal elements that are not phonetically realized, namely, PRO and pro. Let us consider PRO for the purpose of illustration. In LGB this element has a dual nature: it is an anaphor and a pronominal. We will see in chapter 2 that this dual characterization will prevent PRO from appearing in governed positions; that is, PRO may not appear as a constituent of a major XP category—such as VP, NP, or PP—or as subject of a tensed clause. (The notion "government" will be defined in section 2.3.1.) Consider now the following representation:

(9)
John$_i$ was forced t_i [PRO$_i$ to hit Bill]

In the embedded clause of (9) PRO receives the θ-role of agent. This θ-role is different from the one assigned to the controller of PRO, namely, *John*.

I would like to suggest that the middle construction in French illustrates the case of an overt anaphor that does not bear an independent θ-role—in other words, that it instantiates case (8b). In this construction the normal object appears in subject position, the verb is in the active form and agrees with the subject, and the reflexive pronoun *se* is attached to the verb:

(10)
ce livre$_i$ se$_i$ vend bien
'this book sells (itself) well'

Assuming the analysis of these constructions suggested in Williams 1981a, middle constructions display the same characteristics as passive constructions: specifically, the object does not receive a Case-feature within VP, and the subject does not receive a θ-role. In Aoun 1979, Jaeggli 1982, and Borer 1984, it is suggested that clitics absorb Case. (I capitalize *Case* when it stands for *Case-feature*.) Assuming that the nonreferential reflexive clitic absorbs objective Case in (10), the referential NP must end up in subject position, where it receives Case. This is forced by Case theory, which requires every lexical NP to have Case (Rouveret and Vergnaud 1980, LGB). As Williams argues, the syntactic representation of (10) will thus be as follows:

(11)
ce livre$_i$ [$_{VP}$ se$_i$ vend t_i bien]

It is irrelevant for the purpose of our discussion whether middle constructions are generated by a lexical rule or a syntactic rule. Representation (11) seems to capture the basic characteristics of this construction: the surface subject has the θ-role of the object since it is coindexed with it, the subject position itself receives no θ-role, and the verb bears a reflexive clitic.

Since the nonreferential *se* is an anaphor, it must be bound by the subject position, and since the subject position is not a position to which a θ-role is assigned, the referential element in subject position must be coindexed with the object position in order to receive its θ-role. This is required by the θ-Criterion, a well-formedness condition on the distribution of θ-roles that requires every referential element to bear a θ-role and every θ-role to be assigned to one and only one referential element. This well-formedness condition, part of the θ-theory, will be discussed in detail in chapter 2 (see especially section 2.10). Incidentally, the θ-Criterion explains why the reflexive *se* in (11) must be nonreferential. Since there is but one θ-role to be assigned and since the surface subject is a referential element, it must receive the unique θ-role. If *se* were to be referential, two distinct elements would share a unique θ-role, thus violating the θ-Criterion.

The characterization of *se* as a nonreferential element follows from the θ-Criterion. Moreover, as Williams points out, the characterization of *se* as an anaphor follows from the binding requirements. A pronominal clitic such as *le* cannot occur instead of the anaphoric *se*. The reason is that the binding theory would require this pronoun to be disjoint from the antecedent *ce livre:*

(12)
*ce livre$_i$ le$_i$ vend bien
'this book sells it well'

It thus appears that middle constructions illustrate case (8b): *se* is an overt anaphor that does not bear an independent θ-role.

At this point, it is interesting to wonder whether $\overline{\text{A}}$-anaphors may also be classified with respect to the features [$\pm\theta$-role, $\pm$overt]. In section 1.1 we discussed an instance of an overt $\overline{\text{A}}$-anaphor that bears an independent θ-role: *l'altro,* which thus instantiates case (8a). In the following chapters we will see that cases (8b–d) are also instantiated for $\overline{\text{A}}$-anaphors. Case (8d) is instantiated by *wh*-traces or variables (chapter 2). Case (8c) is instantiated by the gap coindexed with the clitic (chapter 4). Finally, case (8b) will be instantiated in existential constructions, as discussed in chapter 5 where various instances of $\overline{\text{A}}$-anaphors are analyzed.

1.3 The Organization of the Grammar

We have seen that the distribution of various nominal expressions may be accounted for by the interaction of three theories: bounding theory, government theory, and binding theory. We have also encountered two other theories constraining syntactic representations: Case theory, which requires every NP to have Case, and the θ-Criterion—part of the θ-theory—which is a uniqueness condition on the assignment of θ-roles:

(13)
a. Bounding theory (includes Subjacency)
b. Government theory (includes the Empty Category Principle)
c. Binding theory (includes the binding principles)
d. θ-theory (includes the θ-Criterion)
e. Case theory

In the following chapters we will examine these theories and their interaction in detail. Together they constrain the distribution of nominal expressions generated by the following system of rules:

(14)
a. Lexicon
b. Syntax
   i. Base rules
   ii. Transformational component
c. Phonetic Form (PF) component
d. Logical Form (LF) component

The Lexicon specifies the abstract morphophonological structures of each lexical item, its categorial features and its contextual features. The form of the base rules is constrained by the X-bar theory (Chomsky 1970). Base rules and lexical insertion rules generate deep structures (D-structures). These structures are mapped into S-structures by the rule Move α, leaving empty categories—traces—bearing the same index as their antecedents. Move α, which constitutes the transformational component, may also apply in the two interpretive components: the PF component and the LF component. The Syntax thus generates S-structures. S-structures are in turn mapped into PF and LF, yielding

Surface-structures and LF-structures, respectively. The organization of the various components of the grammar is represented visually as follows:

(15)

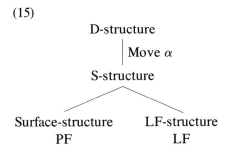

Chapter 2
A Generalized Binding Theory

Since the binding theory appears to constrain $\bar{A}$-anaphoric relations as well as A-anaphoric relations, it is necessary to generalize the binding theory from a theory of A-binding to a theory of A-binding and $\bar{A}$-binding. This is the main purpose of this chapter.

The chapter may be divided in two parts. In sections 2.1 through 2.8 some empirical and conceptual problems in the GB framework will be discussed. The empirical problems involve the extraction of *wh*-elements from inside an NP, which seems to indicate—contrary to what is assumed in GB theory—that the Specified Subject Condition applies to *wh*-traces or variables. The conceptual problems involve some redundancies between the binding theory and the Empty Category Principle.

Generalizing the binding theory to a theory of A-binding and $\bar{A}$-binding will overcome the empirical problems. *Wh*-traces will be treated as $\bar{A}$-anaphors and as namelike expressions. Essentially, it will follow that a *wh*-trace or a variable must be A-free and $\bar{A}$-bound in its governing category: it needs an antecedent in an $\bar{A}$-position, not in an A-position. *Wh*-traces will therefore illustrate a case of nonovert anaphors that have an independent θ-role.

A radical way of avoiding the conceptual problems will be to eliminate the Empty Category Principle (ECP) as an independent principle in the grammar. The generalized binding theory will account for the cases of variables covered by the ECP, and, as indicated in the second part of the chapter (sections 2.10 and 2.11), the θ-Criterion will account for the cases of NP-traces covered by the ECP.

2.1 The Government-Binding Approach

The binding theory as developed in Chomsky 1980 (henceforth, OB) characterizes two domains as opaque in the sense that an anaphor (trace, reciprocal, reflexive, etc.) cannot be free in these domains and a pronoun is disjoint in reference from an "antecedent" within them. The two opaque domains are (a) the subject of a tensed sentence (the Nominative Island Condition: NIC) and (b) the c-command domain of the subject of an NP or S (the Specified Subject Condition: SSC). Among the considerations that motivated the reformulation of the binding principles in LGB are those concerning the behavior of *wh*-traces. L. Rizzi (1982a) indicates that in languages such as Italian that tolerate certain violations of the *Wh*-Island Constraint—namely, those that follow from taking only $\bar{S}$, not S, to be a bounding node for Subjacency—the SSC does not hold for *Wh*-Movement:

(1)
tuo fratello, a cui$_i$ mi domando [che storie abbiano raccontato t_i], era molto preoccupato
'your brother, to whom$_i$ I wonder [which stories they told t_i], was very troubled'

In (1) the *wh*-phrase *a cui* moves in a single step to its S-structure position from the position marked by the trace *t*, violating the SSC. A similar observation can be made in French (where $\bar{S}$, but not S, counts as a bounding node (Sportiche 1981)) with respect to the following sentence, where the movement of the abstract *wh*-element α also violates the SSC:

(2)
c'est à Paul [α_i que Marie sait [quoi donner t_i]]
'it is to Paul that Marie knows what to give'

This appears very natural in light of the similarity between variables and names, as illustrated for example under the condition of strong crossover in the sense of Wasow 1979. Moreover, as pointed out in Freidin and Lasnik 1981, this similarity extends to the domain of Tense—that is, to the NIC. In (3) the variable cannot be coindexed with the pronoun *he*:

(3)
a. who did he say [Mary kissed *t*]
b. who did he say [*t* kissed Mary]

In this respect, the NIC and the SSC are alike: neither applies to variables, which behave in the manner of names in these constructions. Nevertheless, *Wh*-Movement does appear to observe the NIC. That is,

Wh-Movement out of a clause is impossible from the nominative subject position in constructions in which *Wh*-Movement is possible from the domain of a subject. For example, compare (1) and (2) with (4):

(4)

*les hommes, $\begin{bmatrix} \text{que} \\ \text{qui} \end{bmatrix}_i$ je me demande [quelles histoires t_i ont racontées à ton frère], étaient très troublés

'the men, who$_i$ I wonder [which stories t_i told to your brother], were very troubled'

While examples such as (4) appear to indicate that the NIC holds for the variable left by *Wh*-Movement, example (3b) shows that it does not hold. In brief, although *Wh*-Movement is not constrained by the SSC, it apparently is constrained by the NIC. The fact that the *wh*-trace does not appear to be subject to either the NIC or the SSC in the strong crossover contexts extends the problem. These observations are taken in LGB (section 3.1) (from which the above considerations are drawn) to indicate that the NIC in the OB framework expresses a spurious generalization and that in fact two distinct principles are involved in the category of phenomena that had been classified under the NIC. The NIC is restricted to the cases in which there is complete symmetry between the NIC and the SSC. Thus, variables are exempt from both conditions, whereas NP-trace is subject to both. A distinct principle, the ECP, which requires traces to have a local antecedent or to be the complement of an X^0 category such as V, N, or PP, accounts for the fact that *Wh*-Movement appears to be subject to something like the NIC, as in (4) or (5):

(5)
*who do you think that t_i left

We will return to these matters and examine them in detail.

2.2 Some Problems with Government-Binding

2.2.1 The Specified Subject Condition
Examples (1) and (2) have indicated that the SSC does not hold for *Wh*-Movement. The facts are more complex, however, and some restrictions are needed with respect to the conclusion that this condition does not hold for variables. As indicated in Milner 1982 and Zubizarreta 1979 for French and in Cinque 1980 for Italian, the extraction of

PPs from inside NPs is heavily constrained: only subject PPs can be extracted.

Zubizarreta points out that the characterization of the subject in NPs seems to be determined according to a thematic hierarchy:

(6)
a. possessor (or source)
b. agent
c. theme

Thus, consider the following phrases:

(7)
a. le portrait d'Aristote de Rembrandt de   Pierre
            [theme]   [agent]   [possessor]
   'the portrait of Aristotle of Rembrandt of Pierre'

b. le portrait d'Aristote de Rembrandt
            [theme]   [agent]
   'the portrait of Aristotle of Rembrandt'

c. le portrait d'Aristote
            [theme]
   'the portrait of Aristotle'

According to the thematic hierarchy (6), *de Pierre* will be characterized as the subject in (7a), *de Rembrandt* as the subject in (7b), and *d'Aristote* as the subject in (7c). As illustrated by the following phrases, only subjects can be extracted:

(8)
a.   Pierre, dont$_i$ [le portrait d'Aristote de Rembrandt x_i], . . .
     'Pierre, of whom [the portrait of Aristotle of Rembrandt x_i], . . .'
b.   *Rembrandt, dont$_i$ [le portrait d'Aristote x_i de Pierre], . . .
     'Rembrandt, of whom [the portrait of Aristotle x_i of Pierre], . . .'

(9)
a.   Rembrandt, dont$_i$ [le portrait d'Aristote x_i], . . .
     'Rembrandt, of whom [the portrait of Aristotle x_i], . . .'
b.   *Aristote, dont$_i$ [le portrait x_i de Rembrandt], . . .
     'Aristotle, of whom [the portrait x_i of Rembrandt], . . .'

(10)
Aristote, dont$_i$ [le portrait x_i], . . .
'Aristotle, of whom [the portrait x_i], . . .'

Sentences (8) through (10) involve some dialectal variations that need not concern us here (cf. Milner 1982). Note, however, that this hierarchy is at work for *de NP* complements only. As indicated by the ungrammaticality of (12a–b), which are to be contrasted with (10) or (11a–b), other prepositional phrases cannot be subject; therefore, they cannot be extracted:

(11)

a. una persona di cui$_i$ apprezziamo [$_{NP}$ la grande generosità x_i] è Georgio

b. une personne dont$_i$ nous apprécions [la grande générosité x_i] est Georges

'a person of whom$_i$ we appreciate [the great generosity x_i] is George'

(12)

a. *un pianeta su cui$_i$ molti di noi vedranno [$_{NP}$ l'atterraggio x_i] . . .

b. *une planète sur laquelle$_i$ plusieurs d'entre nous verront [l'atterrissage x_i] . . .

'a planet on which$_i$ many of us will see [the landing x_i] . . .'

Assuming as in Vergnaud 1974 that *de NP* complements are real NPs and not PPs—in other words, that *de* is simply a Case-marker—it is possible to say that the thematic hierarchy is at work for NPs but not for PPs: inside an NP only NPs can be subjects.

With this in mind, let us return to sentences (11a–b) and (12a–b), which represent cases of *Wh*-Movement. In (11a–b) the subject—*di cui* in (11a) and *dont* in (11b)—is extracted by *Wh*-Movement and the sentences are grammatical. In (12a–b) the nonsubject—*su cui* in (12a) and *sur laquelle* in (12b)—is also extracted by *Wh*-Movement; the result, however, is ungrammatical. As indicated in Cinque 1980 and Milner 1982, it is tempting to account for the contrast between (11) and (12) in terms of the SSC. Assuming with Cinque that a covert subject is present when an overt one is not, the subject—whether covert or not—or more precisely the SSC will prevent the extraction of the PP in (12). But this constraint will be inoperative in (11).

We are thus led to a near contradiction. Whereas (1) and (2) indicate that the SSC does not hold for variables, (11) and (12) indicate that it does. The situation is therefore similar to the one discussed in section 2.1 where the NIC appears to hold for variables in some cases but not in others.[1] It is true that the SSC seems to hold for variables left by extraction from an NP level but not from a sentential level. The situation is more complex, however, since the LF extraction of *wh*-elements from inside an NP is not constrained by the SSC in English:

(13)
who criticized [$_{NP}$ his writing of which book]

Assuming that Move α in LF raises the *wh*-quantifier and adjoins it to a COMP filled with a *wh*-element (Chomsky 1973, Kayne 1981c, and Aoun, Hornstein, and Sportiche 1981), the movement will violate the SSC:[2]

(14)
[who$_i$, of which book$_j$ [x_i criticized [his writing x_j]]]

2.2.2 Some Conceptual Problems

The GB framework as presented in Chomsky 1979 (PL) and LGB faces other problems as well, which are more conceptual in nature. Although this approach improves upon the one outlined in OB, these problems and the one we have just examined concerning the SSC suggest that some modifications are in order.

The first problem concerns redundancy in the system, specifically between the binding theory and the ECP. Both the binding principles and the ECP require an antecedent for the trace left by NP-Movement: principle (A) of the binding theory requires the NP-trace, an anaphor, to have a c-commanding antecedent in its governing category, and the ECP also requires a c-commanding antecedent (or a lexical governor). These requirements will be discussed in detail later on.

This redundancy does not hold throughout between the two theories. For traces left by *Wh*-Movement (i.e., for variables), the binding theory and the ECP are complementary. The former requires variables to be A-free (not to be c-commanded by an element in an A-position), and the latter requires them to be $\bar{\text{A}}$-bound (to have a c-commanding antecedent in an $\bar{\text{A}}$-position or a lexical governor). The binding theory being a theory of A-binding and not of $\bar{\text{A}}$-binding (i.e., a theory concerned with the relation between elements in A-position), the redundancy is avoided.

The second problem concerns the naturalness of principles and definitions such as the ECP and definition (15) below that single out different occurrences of the same type. In the presentation of GB theory given in PL, the phonetically unrealized pronominal element, PRO, is distinguished from NP-trace and *wh*-trace in that it bears a collection of features (person, number, gender). In chapter 6 of LGB, however, this distinction is no longer maintained. PRO, NP-trace, and *wh*-trace are viewed as three different occurrences of one type, call it *F*. In this approach, the existence of a principle such as the ECP that singles out two occurrences of *F*, NP-trace and *wh*-trace, is not as natural as it is in the presentation given in Pisa. Moreover, the situation is complicated by the existence of definition (15), which singles out in a different way two other occurrences of F, trace and PRO:

(15)
If α is an F, and not a variable, then it is an anaphor.

Although this state of affairs may be inevitable, any attempt to eliminate the ECP or to generalize (15) so as to eliminate the restriction concerning variables, as in (16), is no doubt welcome:

(16)
If α is an F, then it is an anaphor.

GB theory as presented in PL and in LGB recognized the existence of only three empty elements: PRO, NP-trace, and *wh*-trace. The distinction between PRO—a nonovert pronominal anaphoric element—and pro—a nonovert pronominal element—was introduced in Chomsky 1982. For the purpose of the previous discussion, in particular definitions (15) and (16), I have assumed the earlier discussion of empty elements. I will return to pro in section 3.5.2 and incorporate it into the typology of empty categories.

The third problem is more technical in nature and involves the naturalness of the class of proper governors, $[+V^0]$ and NP, singled out by the ECP. In the GB framework the distribution of variables is constrained by the ECP, which requires empty elements to have a local antecedent (NP) or to be properly governed by a lexical element. For the core cases, the lexical elements are nouns (N^0) and verbs (V^0). Now consider the extraction of *wh*-elements from inside an NP. As illustrated in the preceding section, this extraction is limited: only the subject in an NP may be extracted in Italian and French. This may be partially accounted for if it is assumed that nouns (N^0) are not proper governors:

(17)

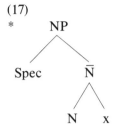

(where the variable x is not a subject)

Since nouns are not proper governors, the variable left by *Wh*-Movement in (17) will not be properly governed; the derivation will be ruled out by the ECP. The extraction of subjects will involve a specific mechanism (to be treated at length in the following sections) whose effect is to provide a "proper governor" for the variable. In short, not all lexical categories but only V^0 (or more precisely $[+V^0]$ elements) and NPs will count as proper governors; the ECP will have to be redefined accordingly. Note, however, that proper governors do not form a natural class. In the literature, various proposals may be thought of as an attempt to overcome the problem (see Kayne 1981b and Jaeggli 1982): in essence, these proposals extend the ECP so as to require an antecedent NP and a governor (V...) for the empty elements. These attempts, however, are subject to the same problem mentioned earlier: they do not avoid the redundancy between the ECP and the binding principles.

2.3 The Binding Theory

To overcome the empirical and conceptual problems mentioned in the preceding two sections, I propose the following solution: generalizing the binding theory from a theory of A-binding to a theory of X-binding (where X = A or $\overline{A}$). Essentially, I will suggest that variables function as anaphors and names and are thus subject to principles (A) (revised) and (C) of the binding theory. Because the change involves crucial use of such fundamental notions as "accessibility" and "governing category," I begin by reviewing these notions and their domain of application as they were originally developed in LGB.

2.3.1 On Government
In the GB framework the notion "government" plays a central role; Case theory, binding theory, and the ECP are formulated in terms of

government. Roughly speaking, Case assignment is a special case of government: it occurs when the governing element happens to be a Case-assigner. The binding principles apply in the domain of the minimal S or NP containing a governor and a governee. The ECP requires empty elements to be properly governed: the proper governors will be a subset of the governors. These principles will be considered more carefully in the following sections.

Government is essentially a relation that holds in a specific structural configuration between a governor and a governed element. In the core case a lexical head governs its complements: the governor is an X^0 element, the governed element is an X, and the structural configuration is as defined in (19) (see Aoun and Sportiche 1983):

(18)
$[_\beta \ldots\gamma\ldots\alpha\ldots\gamma]$ where
a. $\alpha = X^0$
b. where ϕ is a maximal projection, ϕ dominates α iff ϕ dominates γ.

(19)
α governs γ in (18).

2.3.2 The Binding Principles and the Notion "SUBJECT"
In the GB framework nominal expressions are subdivided into three basic categories: anaphors (lexical anaphors, such as reciprocals and reflexives, NP-trace, PRO), pronominals (pro, PRO, and phonetically realized pronouns), and R-expressions (names and variables). The binding theory has one principle for each of these categories:

(20)
Binding Theory
A. An anaphor is bound in its governing category.
B. A pronominal is free in its governing category.
C. An R-expression is free.

The binding is A-binding (antecedent-binding):

(21)
a. α is A-bound by β iff α and β are coindexed, β c-commands α, and β is in an A-position.
b. α is A-free iff it is not A-bound.

To define the notion "governing category," the following rules are assumed (see Emonds 1976):

(22)
S → NP INFL VP
where INFL = [±Tense], [AGR]

AGR(eement) is obligatory with [+Tense] and excluded with [−Tense] in English. The theory also introduces the notion "SUBJECT," which includes the subject of an infinitive, the subject of an NP, and AGR in (22). This notion accords with the idea that the SUBJECT is "the most prominent nominal element" in some sense, taking INFL(ection) to be the head of S. Thus, the italicized elements in (23) are SUBJECTS:

(23)
a. John [$_{INFL}$ past *AGR*] win
b. he wants very much [for *John* to win]
c. he believes [*John* to be intelligent]
d. [*John*'s reading the book] surprised me

In (23b–d) the subject of the embedded phrase is the SUBJECT. In (23a) the subject is *John* and the SUBJECT is *AGR*.

Assuming as in (24) that AGR is coindexed with the NP it governs, *governing category* is defined as in (25):

(24)
AGR is coindexed with the NP it governs.

(25)
β is a *governing category* for α iff β is the minimal category containing α, a governor of α, and a SUBJECT accessible to α.

It follows that β is a governing category only if it has a SUBJECT. Thus, S is always a governing category, and NP is also a governing category when it has a SUBJECT. Principle (24) expresses the phenomenon of agreement. Although AGR creates a governing category in which an anaphor must be bound and a pronominal must be free, AGR is not itself a binder. This accounts for the ungrammaticality of (26a), where the anaphor *each other* is free in its governing category:

(26)
a. *each other win
b. [$_{NP}$ each other] [$_{INFL}$ AGR] [$_{VP}$ win]

As for (25), *accessibility* is defined in terms of the well-formedness condition (27) (the *i*-within-*i* Condition):

(27)

$*[_{\gamma_i} ...\delta_i...]$

(28)

α is *accessible* to β iff β is in the c-command domain of α and coindexing of (α,β) would not violate (27).

The *i*-within-*i* Condition seems to hold for a variety of constructions, as argued in Vergnaud 1974 and Williams 1980:

(29)

a. $*[_{NP_i}$ the friends of $[_{NP_i}$ each other]]

b. *there is $[_{NP_i}$ a picture of $[_{NP_i}$ itself]] on the mantelpiece

c. $*[_{NP_i}$ the owner of $[[_{NP_i}$ his] boat]]

d. $*[_{NP_i}$ the friends of $[[_{NP_i}$ their] parents]]

For the case of an argument within S, the nominative subject of a clause has an accessible SUBJECT: the AGR element of INFL. Hence, the clause is a governing category, within which anaphors must be bound and pronominals must be free:

(30)

a. *they$_i$ said that $[_{S^*}$ each other$_i$ AGR left]

b. *John said that $[_{S^*}$ she$_i$ AGR saw her$_i$]

(where * indicates a governing category)

In the case of an argument within NP, the situation is different: NP is a governing category only when it contains a SUBJECT. For example:

(31)

$[_{S^*}$ we AGR thought $[_S$ that $[_{NP}$ pictures of each other] AGR would be on sale]]

(32)

$[_{S^*}$ *John*$_i$ AGR saw $[_{NP}$ a picture of *him*$_i$]]

In (31) NP contains a governor of *each other* but no SUBJECT accessible to *each other:* the indexing of the embedded AGR and the reciprocal would violate the *i*-within-*i* Condition. Similarly, the embedded S contains a governor of *each other* but not a SUBJECT accessible to *each other*. The matrix S, however, contains a governor of *each other* and a SUBJECT accessible to *each other* (the matrix AGR); it therefore counts as the governing category for the reciprocal *each other* in which it is A-bound by *we,* and the sentence is correctly marked grammatical.

In (32) the governing category for the pronoun is S; it contains a governor of *him* and a SUBJECT accessible to this pronoun (AGR). Binding principle (B) will correctly exclude (32), since the pronoun *him* is bound in its governing category.

Finally, the notion "governing category" must be extended for governed anaphors that lack governing categories because there is no SUBJECT accessible to them:

(33)
*[for each other to win] would be unfortunate

As suggested by N. Hornstein and adopted in LGB (pp. 219–220), root sentences will be considered to count as governing categories for such governed elements. In (33) (noted by L. Rizzi), *each other* has a governing category but no accessible SUBJECT; the main clause counts as its governing category. The anaphor is A-free in this category and the sentence is thus ruled out:

(34)
A root sentence is a governing category for a governed element that lacks an accessible SUBJECT.

2.4 Rearrangement of Government-Binding

In this section I will outline a generalization of the binding principles, suggesting that variables are subject to principles (A) (revised) and (C) of the binding theory. While preserving the fundamental insights embodied in LGB, these modifications may help to solve some of the conceptual and empirical problems mentioned in section 2.2.

2.4.1 X-Binding
Consider the following sentence:

(35)
who [t was killed t']

The trace t is a variable with a Case-feature (Case); we will say that it is *non-argument-bound* ($\bar{A}$-*bound*) by *who*. The trace t' is an anaphor lacking Case; we will say that it is *antecedent-bound* (A-*bound*) by the variable t. Antecedent binding (A-binding) relates an anaphor to an element in A-position. Nonargument binding ($\bar{A}$-binding) relates a variable to an element in $\bar{A}$-position. (Recall that a structural position that receives a grammatical function (subject-of, object-of, etc.) is an argument position; otherwise, it is a nonargument position.)

Two relations—A-binding and $\overline{\text{A}}$-binding—are thus distinguished. The former holds when the binder is in an A-position, and the latter when it is in an $\overline{\text{A}}$-position. A trace in S is an anaphor if it is A-bound and a variable if it is $\overline{\text{A}}$-bound. Like NP-trace, a variable must be bound by a c-commanding antecedent. For variables, however, the antecedent is in an $\overline{\text{A}}$-position and not an A-position, and the theory of binding in (21) must therefore be generalized as follows from A-binding to X-binding (A- or $\overline{\text{A}}$-binding):

(36)
a. α is X-bound by β iff α and β are coindexed, β c-commands α, and β is in an X-position.
b. α is X-free iff it is not X-bound.
c. α is locally bound by β iff α is X-bound by β, and if γ Y-binds α, then either γ Y-binds β or $\gamma = \beta$.
d. α is locally X-bound by β iff α is locally bound and X-bound by β.

(where $\begin{Bmatrix} (X) \\ (Y) \end{Bmatrix} = \text{A or } \overline{\text{A}}$)

The possibility that an element may be locally A-bound and $\overline{\text{A}}$-bound by two different elements is excluded (see LGB, section 3.2.3). A variable will be defined as follows:

(37)
a. $\alpha = [_{NP}\, e]$.
b. α is in an A-position.
c. There is a β that locally $\overline{\text{A}}$-binds α.

(37a) is too narrow; for instance, it prevents phonetically realized pronouns from being treated as variables (Koopman and Sportiche 1982). In chapter 3 the notion "empty element" will be generalized to include phonetically realized pronouns. In that case, (37a) may be generalized as follows:

(38)
α = an empty element.

2.4.2 The Generalized Binding Theory
With these definitions in mind, we can turn to the reformulation of the binding principles.

We will consider that all empty elements discussed so far in this chapter—PRO, NP-trace, and *wh*-trace—are anaphors; as in section 2.2.2, (15) is generalized to (16):

(15)
If α is an empty element F, and not a variable, then it is an anaphor.

(16)
If α is an empty element F, then it is an anaphor.

As for the binding principles, they may be reformulated as follows:

(39)
Generalized Binding Principles
A. An anaphor must be X-bound in its governing category.
B. A pronominal must be X-free in its governing category.
C. A name must be A-free.
   (where $X = A$ or $\overline{A}$)

As an anaphor, PRO will be subject to principle (A). As a pronominal, it will be subject to principle (B); being subject to principles (A) and (B), it must be ungoverned in order to satisfy both requirements (see LGB). C.-T. J. Huang (1982) argues that the *i*-within-*i* Condition is not relevant for pronouns; hence the contrast between (40) and (41) (cf. section 3.2):

(40)
[$_{S^*}$ we AGR thought that [$_S$[$_{NP}$ pictures of each other] AGR would be on sale]]

(41)
[$_S$ we AGR thought that [$_{S^*}$[$_{NP}$ pictures of us] AGR would be on sale]]

As indicated in section 2.3.2, the embedded AGR in (40) is not accessible to *each other* since the indexing of the two elements would violate the *i*-within-*i* Condition. The governing category for the reciprocal is thus the matrix clause: the matrix AGR is accessible to *each other*. Assuming with Huang that the *i*-within-*i* Condition is not relevant for pronouns, the embedded AGR in (41) counts as SUBJECT for *us:* the governing category for this pronoun is the embedded clause. Huang argues that despite this modification, it still follows from the binding theory that PRO is ungoverned. Other avenues can also be explored for deriving the nongovernment requirement concerning PRO. Even though of interest, this need not concern us here; I refer the reader instead to Vergnaud (forthcoming) and Brody 1982. Note in this regard the argument made in Bouchard 1984, Lebeaux 1983, and Sportiche 1983 that in cases of obligatory control, PRO is to be treated as a pure anaphor that may be governed.

Let us turn now to variables. Considered as placeholders for names, as suggested in LGB, they will be subject to binding principle (C), which does not refer to the notion "governing category"; being anaphors, they will be subject to principle (A) as well. The generalized binding theory tries to capture both the insight behind the OB theory according to which variables are treated like anaphors and the insight behind the GB theory according to which variables are namelike elements. Note also that the fact that variables must be $\overline{\text{A}}$-bound and not A-bound seems to follow from their being subject to binding principles (A) and (C). The only way to satisfy both principles is for variables to be $\overline{\text{A}}$-bound. In the following chapters, however, we will encounter instances of overt and nonovert $\overline{\text{A}}$-anaphors that are not subject to principle (C). If such instances exist, the fact that some anaphors must be $\overline{\text{A}}$-bound while others must be A-bound cannot follow from the binding principles. We will return to these considerations in a somewhat different context when we discuss the parallelism between the system of A-anaphoric relations and the system of $\overline{\text{A}}$-anaphoric relations.

Note that in formulating principle (C), I replaced *R-expression* by *name*, in part to avoid the problems of pronouns such as *I, you* that one may be tempted to treat as R-expressions (see section 3.2). This terminological modification is not crucial; the original formulation given in section 2.3.2 could have been kept as well. Recently, the status of principle (C) as an independent principle in the grammar has been questioned, and it has been suggested that its effect may be derived from the interaction of various grammatical rules (see Chomsky 1982, Higginbotham 1983; H. Lasnik argues for an opposite view in a forthcoming work). As will become clear, the effect of this principle—and not its status—is what is important for us.

2.5 Extraction from Ss

Let us now see concretely how the system outline in section 2.4 works.

As mentioned in section 2.1, variables violate the SSC in languages such as Italian and French where $\overline{\text{S}}$, but not S, is taken as a bounding node. An example is (42) (= (2)):

(42)

c'est à Paul [$_{\bar{S}}$ α_i que [$_S$ Marie AGR sait [$_{\bar{S}}$ quoi$_j$ [$_S$ PRO donner x_j x_i]]]]

Consider x_j and x_i. These variables are governed by the verb *donner* but have no accessible SUBJECT. An element in an A-position—such as PRO of the embedded clause—cannot function as an accessible SUBJECT for a variable. This possibility is excluded by principle (C) of the (generalized) binding theory: the variable would end up being A-bound if we were to assign to it the index of the SUBJECT in A-position. Thus, the notion "accessibility" defined in (28) is to be reformulated as follows:

(43)

α is *accessible* to β iff β is in the c-command domain of α and coindexing of (α,β) would not violate the *i*-within-*i* Condition (27) or principle (C) of the binding theory.

Definition (43) can presumably be generalized to (44):

(44)

α is *accessible* to β iff β is in the c-command domain of α and coindexing of (α,β) would not violate any grammatical principle.

For our purposes, it is enough to keep in mind that the *i*-within-*i* Condition and binding principle (C) cannot be violated. One may think prima facie that generalizing the definition of accessibility given in (28) to (43) or (44) renders the system circular: the notion "accessible SUBJECT" serves to define a governing category relevant for the formulation of the binding principles, and this notion itself refers to the binding principles; it uses something it is supposed to define. This is not so, however. The notion "accessible SUBJECT" makes crucial use of principle (C) of the binding theory; but this principle—contrary to principles (A) and (B)—does not refer to the notion "governing category." The circularity is thus avoided.

In (42) the variables x_i and x_j have a governor *donner* but no accessible SUBJECT. By binding principle (C), PRO cannot function as an accessible SUBJECT. If it is assumed that it is not in an A-position, AGR in the matrix clause by itself can function as an accessible SUBJECT for these variables. However, this AGR is coindexed with the subject, *Marie*. Assuming transitivity of indexing, the variables will end up being A-bound by *Marie,* in violation of the binding theory. Therefore, the matrix AGR cannot function as an accessible SUBJECT. By principle (C), neither AGR nor an element in an A-position can function as an accessible SUBJECT for a variable in nonsubject position. Thus, in general:

(45)
On a sentential level, variables in nonsubject position do not have an accessible SUBJECT.

Note that the following logical possibility exists: AGR may count as accessible SUBJECT for a variable in nonsubject position, if the sentence does not contain any subject. However, subjects on a sentential level are always obligatory. The obligatoriness of subjects in clausal structures follows from the Extended Projection Principle (see LGB, section 2.2). This logical possibility thus does not arise. Since the governed variables x_i and x_j have no accessible SUBJECT, they have no governing category. Recall, however, the discussion of example (33), which necessitated extending the notion "governing category" as in (34): a root sentence counts as a governing category for governed elements that happen to have no accessible SUBJECT. This applies to the governed variables x_j and x_i: their governing category is the main clause. By binding principle (A), they must be $\overline{A}$-bound in this category, which they are: x_j is $\overline{A}$-bound by $quoi_j$ and x_i by α_i. The derivation is therefore well formed.

   If governed variables in nonsubject positions have no accessible SUBJECT, then the main clause functions as their governing category, accounting for the possibility of long cases of Wh-Movement as in (42). The situation is different for variables in subject position, however: nothing prevents the AGR they are coindexed with from functioning as an accessible SUBJECT:

(46)
... x_k AGR$_k$ V

In this light, consider the following pair:

(47)
a. *who$_i$ do you think [$_{\overline{S}_1}$ t_i that [$_{S_1}$ x_i AGR left]]
b. who$_i$ do you think [$_{\overline{S}_1}$ t_i [$_{S_1}$ x_i AGR left]]

In (47) $\overline{S}_1$ is the governing category for the variable x_i: it is the minimal category containing a governor (INFL/AGR) and an accessible SUBJECT (AGR). By binding principle (A), this variable must be $\overline{A}$-bound in $\overline{S}_1$. x_i is $\overline{A}$-bound in (47a) but not in (47b), where the presence of *that* prevents the intermediate trace from locally binding the variable. Therefore, (47a) but not (47b) is correctly marked ungrammatical.

In section 2.7.1 we will consider why the presence of a complementizer such as *that* prevents the trace in COMP from locally binding the variable. Two analyses have been suggested in the literature. The first, suggested for instance in Kayne 1981c and Pesetsky 1982a, considers that the presence of *that* prevents the trace in COMP from c-commanding the variable. The second, suggested in Aoun, Hornstein, and Sportiche 1981, accounts for this phenomenon in terms of a COMP-indexing rule.

Let us now consider some implications of the analysis presented so far. As a consequence of generalizing the binding theory to a theory of X-binding, it is necessary to extend the notion "governing category." Since a variable must be $\bar{\text{A}}$-bound in its governing category (by principle (A) of the generalized binding theory) and since the $\bar{\text{A}}$-binder is generally an element in COMP, it follows that—at least for variables—$\bar{\text{S}}$ and not S is to be taken as a governing category. This is clearly illustrated in the discussion of examples (47a–b), where the embedded $\bar{\text{S}}_1$ is considered as the governing category for variables. If the embedded S_1 were considered as the governing category, the variables would be $\bar{\text{A}}$-free in this S and (47a–b) would both be incorrectly marked ungrammatical. It is legitimate to ask what the consequences of this change are. Is it always possible to consider $\bar{\text{S}}$—and not S—as the governing category?

Under the definition of governing category given in (25), the choice of $\bar{\text{S}}$ instead of S as the governing category for A-anaphors and pronouns is irrelevant. To see why, consider (48):

(48)

$$[_{\bar{S}_1}[_{S_1} \text{ they}_i \text{ AGR prefer } [_{\bar{S}} \text{ for } [_S \begin{bmatrix} \text{each other}_i \\ \text{them}_j \end{bmatrix} \text{ to win}]]]]$$

The governor of the elements in the embedded subject position (*each other* and *them*) is the preposition *for;* the first (accessible) SUBJECT is AGR of the matrix clause. Therefore, the governing category is the matrix clause ($\bar{\text{S}}_1$ or S_1). In this category *each other* must be A-bound to *they* and the pronoun *them* disjoint from *they*.

It thus appears that under the definition of governing category adopted in (25), the choice of $\bar{\text{S}}$ or S as the governing category is irrelevant for A-anaphors and pronominals. For $\bar{\text{A}}$-anaphors, such as variables, on the other hand, $\bar{\text{S}}$ and not S must be chosen as the governing category (recall (47a–b)). We therefore conclude that $\bar{S}$ may always be considered as the governing category. This fact does not need to be stipulated if the definition of governing category is formulated as follows:

(49)
β is a *governing category* for α iff β is the minimal maximal projection containing α, a governor of α, and a SUBJECT accessible to α.

For example, consider (48). As indicated above, the governing category for the elements in the embedded subject position is the matrix clause. Assuming that $\bar{S}$ but not S is a maximal projection, the governing category for *each other* and *them* will be $\bar{S}_1$.

We have seen that generalizing the binding principles triggers other changes: generalizing the notion "accessibility" and choosing $\bar{S}$ and not S as the governing category. As a result, the generalized binding theory is able to handle some cases accounted for in LGB in terms of the ECP (the contrast between (47a) and (47b), for instance). It is therefore legitimate to ask whether this redundancy can be eliminated: given the discussion of the GB framework in sections 2.1 and 2.2, is it possible to dispense with the ECP, at least for variables? I believe so. Before demonstrating how it is to be done, though, I will illustrate the application of the system on an NP-level and indicate that it solves some problems mentioned in sections 2.1 and 2.2.

2.6 Extraction from NPs

As we have seen, the SSC seems to hold for variables left by extraction from NP in Italian and French, though not for variables left by extraction on a sentential level. Consider the following paradigm:

(50)
a.   tu as vu [$_{NP}$ le portrait d'Aristote de Rembrandt]
      'you saw the portrait of Aristotle of (= by) Rembrandt'
b.   l'artiste dont$_i$ tu as vu [$_{NP}$ le portrait d'Aristote x_i]
      'the artist of whom you saw the portrait of Aristotle'
c.   *l'homme dont$_i$ tu as vu [$_{NP}$ le portrait x_i de Rembrandt]
      'the man of whom you saw the portrait of (= by) Rembrandt'

The contrast between (50b) and (50c) illustrates the fact that a subject but not an object can be extracted by *Wh*-Movement. To account for this contrast, we need to assume that the NP is the governing category for the extracted elements in (50b–c) and that in (50b), but not in (50c), the variable is $\overline{\text{A}}$-bound in this governing category. To obtain this result, the following considerations concerning the internal structure of French and Italian will be helpful (I will illustrate using French examples).

First, French exhibits a special relation between the prenominal position and the subject inside an NP: only the subject can be replaced by a prenominal possessive (see Milner 1982 for relevant considerations):

(51)
a. tu as vu le portrait d'Aristote de Rembrandt
b. tu as vu son portrait d'Aristote
    'you saw his portrait of Aristotle'
c. *tu as vu son portrait de Rembrandt
    'you saw his portrait of Rembrandt'

(52)
a. tu as vu le portrait d'Aristote
b. tu as vu son portrait
    'you saw his portrait'

Sentence (51c) is ungrammatical if the possessive is construed as the theme: 'you saw the portrait that Rembrandt made of x'. It is grammatical if the possessive is construed as the owner—'you saw the portrait of Rembrandt that x owns'—or the agent—'you saw the portrait that x made of Rembrandt'. In other words, (51c) is grammatical if, according to the thematic hierarchy (6), the possessive is construed as the subject.

One way of encoding the special relation existing between the prenominal position and the subject inside an NP is to assume that this position and the postnominal subject are coindexed. M.-L. Zubizarreta (1979) suggests (although for different considerations) that the determiner and the subject of an NP are coindexed. My proposal is slightly different in that it does not require the determiner per se to be coindexed with the subject.

The second relevant consideration involves the elements that may appear in prenominal position. R. S. Kayne (personal communication) has noted that in French, contrary to English, a lexical NP cannot appear in prenominal position inside an NP:

(53)

a. *Jean livre

b.   Jean's book

One way to characterize the difference between English and French is to say that the Specifier in English—but not in French—may contain an A-position (Chomsky 1970, Jackendoff 1977). An immediate consequence of this proposal concerns the status of the prenominal position filled by a possessive clitic in French. Since the Specifier does not contain an A-position and since a possessive clitic appears in prenominal position, we conclude that the possessive clitic is in $\bar{A}$-position in French. More generally, it is possible to assume that clitics are generated in $\bar{A}$-positions. (A similar idea concerning clitics has been suggested in an unpublished work by R. Huybregts.) Finally, we will assume that in French the Specifier of the NP counts as the most prominent element (= SUBJECT) with respect to the elements occurring in this NP. In brief, then, we have made the following assumptions concerning the internal structure of the NP in French:

(54)

a. The subject of an NP and the prenominal position are coindexed.

b. The prenominal position is an $\bar{A}$-position.

c. The Specifier is the most prominent element (= SUBJECT) of an NP.

With this in mind, let us return to the contrast between (50b) and (50c). Assuming (54a), these sentences will have the following representations, where (55a) and (55b) correspond to (50b) and (50c), respectively. (For typographical convenience, I assume that the determiner is coindexed with the subject; recall, however, the discussion of sentences (51a–c), (52a–b).)

(55)

a.   l'artiste dont$_i$ tu as vu [$_{NP}$ le$_i$ portrait d'Aristote x_i]

b. *l'homme dont$_i$ tu as vu [$_{NP}$ le$_j$ portrait x_i de Rembrandt$_j$]

The governor of the variable x in (55a–b) is *portrait* and the accessible SUBJECT is the whole Specifier; therefore, the governing category for the variable is NP. The subject variable in (55a) is coindexed with the prenominal position, which is an $\bar{A}$-position; thus, it is $\bar{A}$-bound in its governing category. On the other hand, the nonsubject variable in (55b) is $\bar{A}$-free in its governing category. (55b) violates binding principle (A) since the variable—an $\bar{A}$-anaphor—is not $\bar{A}$-bound in its governing category.

The same analysis accounts for the contrast between (56a) and (56b), pointed out to me by A. Rouveret:

(56)
a.   tu as vu [$_{NP}$ le portrait d'Aristote de quel artiste]
     'you saw the portrait of Aristotle of which artist'
b.   ?*tu as vu [$_{NP}$ le portrait de quel homme de Rembrandt]
     'you saw the portrait of which man of Rembrandt'

Assuming as in (13) that Move α in LF raises the base-generated *wh*-element that did not undergo movement in Syntax and adjoins it to COMP (see Aoun, Hornstein, and Sportiche 1981 for a detailed analysis of these sentences), the respective LF representations of (56a–b) will be similar to (55a–b):

(57)
a.   de quel artiste$_i$ [tu as vu [$_{NP}$ le$_i$ portrait d'Aristote x_i]]
b.   *de quel homme$_i$ [tu as vu [$_{NP}$ le$_j$ portrait x_i de Rembrandt$_j$]]

Again, only in (57a) is the variable $\bar{A}$-bound in its governing category, thus satisfying binding principle (A). Examples such as (56a–b) are of interest in that they show that the binding principles apply in LF—but not necessarily in LF only—since the variable in these examples is generated by an LF rule.

It thus appears that a certain parallelism exists between the extraction of a *wh*-element from S and the extraction of a *wh*-subject from NP. The extraction of a *wh*-element from S proceeds via COMP, which provides an "escape hatch" for this *wh*-element (see Chomsky 1977b for a discussion of this notion). The extraction of a *wh*-subject from an NP is made possible because this subject is coindexed with the prenominal $\bar{A}$-position. Thus, this prenominal position also constitutes an "escape hatch" (for the subject). In this respect, it is interesting to note that whether the subject is extracted via the prenominal position or not is irrelevant, since the prenominal position and the subject are coindexed by assumption (54b).

In summary, it appears that the extraction of *wh*-elements from NPs in French can be accounted for if it is assumed that the NP constitutes an opaque domain—a governing category—in which the variable must be $\bar{A}$-bound. The variable left by the extraction of a subject will be bound by the prenominal $\overline{A}$-position. But the variable left by the extraction of a nonsubject will be free, thus violating the binding theory.

2.6.1 Extraction in Hebrew

A striking confirmation of the analysis just presented is given by the behavior of variables in the construct state in Modern Hebrew. The construct state in Modern Hebrew indicates genitival relations between the head N and the complement, which can be a lexical NP (as in (58a)) or a clitic (as in (58b)). These examples are taken from Borer 1984; they are given there to support the proposal that clitics function as proper governors:

(58)
a. ktivat   Dan
   writing Dan
   'Dan's writing'
b. ktivato
   writing his
   'his writing'

The clitic attached to the head noun can appear with a coreferential NP; in this case, a Case-marker *šel* is inserted in front of that NP. This is another instance of the so-called clitic doubling phenomenon:

(59)
a. ktivato$_i$ šel-Dan$_i$
   writing his of Dan
   'Dan's writing'
b. ktivato$_i$ šel-hasefer$_i$
   writing it of the book
   'the writing of the book'

The NP cooccurring with the clitic can also be disjoint from it, in which case the marker *ʔet* is inserted:

(60)
Dan biker   ʔet ktivato$_i$ ʔet hasefer$_j$
Dan criticized acc writing his acc the book
'Dan criticized his writing of the book'

Now consider the following pair, where the NP cooccurring with the clitic is a *wh*-element:

(61)

a. mi   biker   ʔet ktivato$_i$ šel ʔeize sefer$_i$
    who criticized acc writing it of which book
    'who criticized the writing of which book'

b. *mi   biker   ʔet ktivato$_j$ ʔet ʔeize sefer$_i$
    who criticized acc writing his acc which book
    'who criticized his writing of which book'

The contrast between (61a) and (61b) is similar to the one holding
between (57a) and (57b). Assuming that Move α in LF raises the base-
generated *wh*-element, the LF representation of (61a–b) will be as
follows (irrelevant details omitted):

(62)

a. [for which x_i, x_i a book] . . . [$_{NP}$ N + cl$_i$ x_i]

b. *[for which x_i, x_i a book] . . . [$_{NP}$ N + cl$_j$ x_i]

Once again, this contrast may be accounted for if it is assumed that the
NP constitutes a governing category for the variable and that this variable is $\bar{A}$-bound in (62a)—but not in (62b)—by the clitic. Since the
variable in (62a) bears the same index as the clitic and since clitics are
in $\bar{A}$-positions, it will be $\bar{A}$-bound by this clitic, thus satisfying the
binding theory. In (62b), however, the clitic is disjoint from the variable
and thus does not count as an $\bar{A}$-binder. (62b) will be ruled out by the
binding theory since the variable is free in its governing category.

One question worth exploring at this point concerns the characterization of the position occupied by AGR (or INFL). Note that AGR
does not $\bar{A}$-bind the variable in subject position with which it is coindexed; that is, AGR is not in an $\bar{A}$-position. It cannot be in an
A-position either. This is because it is coindexed with the subject position, which may be filled by a name:

(63)

John$_i$ AGR$_i$ left

If AGR were in an A-position, principle (C) of the binding theory would
be violated: *John* would be A-bound by AGR. I am assuming that the
indexing between the subject and AGR is of the same nature as the
indexing between an anaphor and its antecedent or a pronoun and its
antecedent (see Safir 1982 for relevant discussion of the indexing
mechanisms available in the grammar). Thus, AGR is neither in an
A-position nor in an $\bar{A}$-position. It is possible to suggest that head-

positions in general are neither A- nor Ā-positions. This amounts to saying that there are three kinds of positions in the grammar: A-positions, Ā-positions, and head-positions. The first two positions are generally XP-positions, the last is generally an X^0-position. For instance:

(64)

In (64) the NP is an A-position with respect to the V; the V is the head-position. As indicated in section 2.3.1, the head-position is relevant for government. Basically, the head-position governs the XP-positions contained in the maximal projection of this head. It is therefore relevant for Case assignment and thematic assignment, which occur in a government context.

2.6.2 Noun Phrases in English

From the previous French and Hebrew examples, it appears that the extraction of a *wh*-element from inside an NP can be accounted for by the binding theory if it is assumed that NP in these languages constitutes an opaque domain in which the variable left by *wh*-extraction must be bound. However, this cannot always be the case; there are languages where NP is not systematically an opaque domain. Consider the following English example (see note 2):

(65)
who criticized [NP his writing of which book]

After Move α applies in LF, the representation of (65) will be as follows (irrelevant details omitted):

(66)
[s̄ who, of which book$_i$ . . . [NP his writing x_i]]

If the NP were to count as an opaque domain—if, for instance, *his* were an accessible SUBJECT—the sentence would incorrectly be ruled out as ungrammatical: the variable is Ā-free in its governing category. The fact that *his* may not count as an accessible SUBJECT for the variable in (66) is presumably to be related to the fact that the pronoun in English is in an A-position and by the binding principle (C) cannot function as an accessible SUBJECT for the variable since this variable would end up being A-bound. We then expect that when a variable is replaced by a reciprocal, *his* may function as an accessible SUBJECT since binding principle (C) is irrelevant for reciprocals. This expectation is fulfilled:

(67)
*they like [$_{NP}$ his pictures of each other]

In (67) NP is the governing category for *each other;* it contains the governor *pictures* and an accessible SUBJECT, *his.* The derivation is ruled out since the reciprocal is A-free in its governing category. (67), where the governing category is NP, contrasts with (66), where the governing category is the whole clause: the difference is that in (66), contrary to (67), *his* cannot function as a SUBJECT accessible to the variable. Thus, in (66) x has a governor but no accessible SUBJECT. By the extension of the notion "governing category" adopted in (34), the root clause will count as governing category for the variable. In this clause, the variable is $\bar{A}$-bound.

Finally, consider the following sentence:

(68)
they$_i$ like [$_{NP}$ the pictures of each other$_i$]

If, as in French, the Specifier in (68) were to count as an accessible SUBJECT, the NP would be the governing category for the reciprocal and the sentence would incorrectly be ruled out as ungrammatical since *each other* would be free in the NP. It thus appears that in English the NP counts as a governing category for a reciprocal only when the pre-nominal A-position is filled by a lexical element, as in (67): the Specifier in English, unlike the Specifier in French, does not count as SUBJECT. It is the A-position of the Specifier in English that counts as SUBJECT.

If this is so, we expect the French sentence corresponding to (68) to be ungrammatical:

(69)
*ils aiment [$_{NP}$ les photos l'un de l'autre]

This is indeed the case. The contrast between (68) and (69) is to be expected if the Specifier in French—but not in English—counts as an accessible SUBJECT: the NP in (69) will be the governing category and the binding theory will correctly rule the sentence ungrammatical since the anaphor *l'un de l'autre* will be A-free in its governing category.[3]

A similar situation exists in Italian. Recall that two anaphoric relations are at work in the reciprocal constructions of Italian: (R1), the anaphoric relation between *l'uno* and *l'altro,* and (R2), the anaphoric relation between *l'uno* and an antecedent. (R1) is an $\overline{\text{A}}$-anaphoric relation: *l'uno* is the $\overline{\text{A}}$-binder of *l'altro.* (R2) is an A-anaphoric relation: the antecedent of *l'uno* is in an A-position. With this in mind, consider the contrast between (70a) and (70b), which was used in section 1.1 to indicate that (R1) is constrained by the binding theory:

(70)
a.   quei reporters ammiravano l'uno [$_{NP}$ le foto dell'altro]
     'those reporters admired each other's pictures'
b.   *quei reporters ammiravano l'uno [$_{NP}$ le tue foto dell'altro]
     'those reporters admired one your pictures of the other'

The facts just illustrated for French also hold for Italian: NP constitutes an opaque domain—a governing category—in which an anaphor must be bound, and the prenominal position is an $\overline{\text{A}}$-position coindexed with the subject of the NP. It thus is able to $\overline{\text{A}}$-bind this subject. In (70a–b) NP constitutes an opaque domain—a governing category. In (70a) the subject *dell'altro* is $\overline{\text{A}}$-bound by the prenominal position in its governing category. In (70b), however, *dell'altro* is not the subject of the NP; it is not coindexed with the prenominal position. (70b) violates the binding requirement: the anaphor *dell'altro* is free in its governing category.

A similar analysis holds for (71):

(71)
*Mario e Francesco ammiravano l'uno [$_{NP}$ i libri sull'altro]
'Mario and Francesco admire one the book about the other'

Here the governing category for the $\overline{\text{A}}$-anaphor *sull'altro* is the NP. Since the anaphor *sull'altro* is not the subject of the NP, it will not be coindexed with the prenominal position. (71) will be excluded like (70b) by binding principle (A): the $\overline{\text{A}}$-anaphor is free in its governing category.

This account correctly predicts that the binding theory will also rule out sentences like (72):

(72)
*hanno visto [$_{NP}$ le foto l'uno dell'altro]
'they saw the pictures of each other'

Here too, the governing category for the A-anaphor *l'uno* is the NP. In this NP, *l'uno* is not A-bound. Therefore, (72) will be excluded by binding principle (A).[4]

Thus, (70b), (71), and (72) will be excluded by the binding theory. (70b) and (71) will be excluded because the $\overline{\text{A}}$-anaphor *l'altro* is not bound in its governing category, the NP. (72) will be excluded because the A-anaphor *l'uno* is free in its governing category. The analysis suggested in section 2.6 concerning the extraction of elements from inside an NP therefore extends to the distribution of reciprocal expressions in this NP: it correctly distinguishes between the behavior of A-anaphors and the behavior of $\overline{\text{A}}$-anaphors inside NPs. It thus provides further evidence for the analysis suggested in section 2.6 and for the distinction between the two kinds of relations relevant for the binding theory: A-binding and $\overline{\text{A}}$-binding.

From our comparison of English and French, then, we can see that what counts as SUBJECT apparently admits some degree of parametric variation across languages. It is interesting to point out that this parametrization seems to exist not only across languages but also between speakers of the same language:

(73)
they found [$_{NP}$ some books [$_{\bar{S}}$ for each other to read]]

Most speakers tend to regard this sentence as grammatical; others reject it. A way of accounting for this dialectal difference may be to consider, as suggested in PL, that for speakers who permit binding of *each other* by *they, some* (or *some books*) does not count as an (accessible) SUBJECT, thus allowing the main clause to be the governing category. For speakers who consider (73) ungrammatical, *some* (or *some books*) counts as an accessible SUBJECT. In this case NP will be the governing category and the reciprocal will be A-free in this governing category, thus violating the binding principles.

What counts as accessible SUBJECT may vary in a language not only from speaker to speaker but also with respect to the nature of the element subject to the binding theory. Thus, D. Godard (1980) notes the following contrast:

(74)
a. *le livre que je ne sais pas si les élèves verront
   'the book that I don't know whether the students will see'
b. le film auquel je ne sais pas si je pourrai assister
   'the movie that I don't know whether I will be able to see'

The extraction of a *wh*-NP out of a tensed clause headed by a complementizer such as *si* 'whether' is ungrammatical, as in (74a). However, the extraction of a *wh*-PP is grammatical, as in (74b). In other words, a tensed clause headed by *si* constitutes an opaque domain for a *wh*-NP but not a *wh*-PP. This fact is peculiar to French. As Godard notes, it does not hold in another language similar to French where S̄ (but not S) is also taken as a bounding node—namely, Italian. It indicates that *si* in French tensed clauses functions as the most prominent element—accessible SUBJECT—with respect to *wh*-NPs, but not *wh*-PPs. Although it is of interest, I will not pursue here the parametric variation concerning what counts as SUBJECT. Some relevant considerations concerning this question are to be found in Aoun (to appear).

To review: we are now assuming a generalized binding theory applying in LF at least and incorporating definition (16) and the binding principles given in (39). The notion "governing category" is defined as in (49) in terms of accessibility (43). This theory yields the positive results of the earlier version of the binding theory restricted to a theory of A-binding and accommodates a complex range of cases such as the behavior of variables in NPs (cf. the French, Italian, and Hebrew examples discussed above) that the earlier version cannot naturally account for. The new theory also seems to handle some cases accounted for in terms of the ECP in LGB. It remains to see whether the redundancy between the binding theory and the ECP can be eliminated from the system. I will first discuss constructions where the variable violates the ECP and then constructions where the NP-trace violates the ECP.

2.7 The Empty Category Principle

From the binding theory as formulated in LGB, it follows that a variable, while Ā-bound by definition, is A-free and thus exempt from any effect of the NIC or the SSC, these being theorems of the binding theory. Variables are therefore similar to names with regard to the binding theory.

We have seen that variables in some cases violate the NIC (ex. (3a)) and the SSC (exs. (1) and (2)), though there are also cases where variables appear to obey the SSC (exs. (8) through (10)). This led to reformulating the binding principles and extending principle (A) to all empty categories including variables. We have also noted that the conclusion that variables do not obey the NIC is problematic because in other respects they do seem to obey this condition (see (5)): structure

(75) is excluded if ... is nonnull, where t is nominative and is the variable bound by α:

(75)

*$[_{\bar{S}} \alpha \ldots [_S t \text{ INFL VP}]]$

This seems prima facie to be a violation of the NIC. Examples include indirect questions, *that*-trace effects, and the Superiority Condition, illustrated in (76a–c), respectively:

(76)

a. *who$_i$ do you wonder $[_{\bar{S}}$ how $[_S t_i$ solved the problem]]
b. *who$_i$ do you think $[_{\bar{S}} t_i$ that $[_S t_i$ saw Bill]]]
c. *it is unclear $[_{\bar{S}}$ what $[_S$ who saw $t]]$

In (76a) the trace t is $\overline{\text{A}}$-bound by *who*, and in (76b) it is bound by *who* or perhaps by a trace in the embedded COMP (t *that*). Similarly in (76c), if we assume that a movement rule in the LF component adjoins *who* to its COMP, giving the LF representation (77). (77) contrasts with the grammatical example (78), which has the LF representation (79). (We will return to these sentences.)

(77)

it is unclear $[_{\bar{S}}[_{\text{COMP}}$ who$_i$ $[_{\text{COMP}}$ what$_j$]] $[_S t_i$ saw $t_j]]$

(78)

it is unclear $[_{\bar{S}}$ who$_i$ $[t_i$ saw what]]

(79)

it is unclear $[_{\bar{S}}[_{\text{COMP}}$ what$_j$ $[_{\text{COMP}}$ who$_i$]] $[_S t_i$ saw $t_j]]$

Examples in (76a–c), then, are cases of (75), and they appear to show that variables are indeed subject to the NIC. In LGB (section 4.1) the phenomenon illustrated in (75), while similar to the NIC effects, is treated as a separate phenomenon, referred to as the *RES(NIC)* (Residue of the NIC). Some other principle is involved in RES(NIC), a phenomenon that holds at the level of LF representation rather than S-structure, if (76c) does belong to this complex. The relevant principle is the ECP; it requires traces to be properly governed in LF.

To define proper government, the notion of government is extended. In section 2.3.1 governors were restricted to elements of the form X^0 of the X-bar system: $[\pm N, \pm V]^0$. For proper government, it is assumed that a coindexed NP in COMP may be a governor for the ECP:

(80)

$[_\beta \ldots\gamma\ldots\alpha\ldots\gamma\ldots]$ where:

a. $\alpha = X^0$ or is coindexed with γ

b. where ϕ is a maximal projection, if ϕ dominates γ, then ϕ dominates α.

(81)

α governs γ in (80).

Proper government is defined in (82), and the ECP is formulated in (83):

(82)

α *properly governs* β iff α governs β and α is lexical.

(83)

An empty category must be properly governed.

Recall, however, that not all X^0 categories are proper governors; only $[+V]^0$ elements seem to be. In fact, R. S. Kayne (1981b) has shown that Ns and Ps are not proper governors. If this is so, (82) will have to be redefined accordingly:

(84)

α *properly governs* β iff α governs β and α is $[+V]^0$ or NP.

The similarity between the Superiority Condition and the other RES(NIC) phenomena (cf. (76)) provides some reason to suspect that the ECP holds for all variables at the level of LF. Some direct evidence that the ECP holds for variables formed by LF rules, hence at the level of LF, are provided in Kayne 1981c (also see Aoun, Hornstein, and Sportiche 1981). Consider sentences (85a–b):

(85)

a.   I don't remember which man said that John saw which woman

b.   ?*I don't remember which man said that which woman saw John

Assuming as before the existence of the LF rule that moves the *wh*-phrase *which woman* to a COMP containing a *wh*-phrase, the LF representations of (85a–b) will be as follows (irrelevant details omitted):

(86)

a.   ... $[_{\bar{S}_1}[_{COMP}$ which woman$_i$ $[_{COMP}$ which man$_j$]] $[_{S_1} x_j$ said $[_{\bar{S}_0}$ that $[_S$ John saw $x_i]]]]$

b.   ... $[_{\bar{S}_1}[_{COMP}$ which woman$_i$ $[_{COMP}$ which man$_j$]] $[_{S_1} x_j$ said $[_{\bar{S}_0}$ that $[_{S_0} x_i$ saw John]]]]$

The contrast between (86a) and (86b) may be accounted for by the ECP since the variable x_i in (86b)—but not in (86a)—is not properly governed. Thus, despite the conceptual problems mentioned in section 2.2, the ECP achieves a considerable level of empirical and explanatory adequacy: it accounts in a unified way for such different phenomena as multiple interrogation (ex. (85)), the *[that-t] effect (ex. (76b)), and the Superiority Condition (ex. (76c)). Recall, however, that at least for the *[that-t] effect (exs. (47a–b)), the ECP seems to be redundant with the generalized binding principles. We will attempt to eliminate this redundancy, but first let us consider in detail some of the constructions that obey the ECP.

Despite the remarks in the previous paragraphs, it is not obvious how superiority is to be accounted for by the ECP since at the relevant level (LF) the variable in subject position is not c-commanded by *who* in (77) and (79) (repeated in (87) and (88), respectively):

(87)

it is unclear [$_\bar{S}$[COMP who$_i$ [COMP what$_j$]] [$_S$ t_i saw t_j]]

(88)

it is unclear [$_\bar{S}$[COMP what$_j$ [COMP who$_i$]] [$_S$ t_i saw t_j]]

Both (87) and (88) will incorrectly be ruled out by the ECP since the variable t_i is not c-commanded by the operator *who*. In other words, we expect (87) and (88) to be excluded for the same reason as (76b), repeated in (89):

(89)

*who$_i$ do you think [$_\bar{S}$ t_i that [t_i saw Bill]]

A solution for what appears to be merely a technical problem is to assume that the movement rule in LF that raises the *wh*-quantifier adjoins this quantifier to $\bar{S}$-marked [+wh]. This can be technically achieved if it is assumed that COMP/INFL form a discontinuous head and that the features of the head percolate up to the projection ($\bar{S}$) of the head. This idea concerning COMP/INFL is suggested in Aoun 1979.

(90)

it is unclear [$_\bar{S}$ who$_i$ [$_\bar{S}$[COMP what$_j$] [$_S$ t_i saw t_j]]]

(91)

it is unclear [$_\bar{S}$ what$_j$ [$_\bar{S}$[COMP who$_i$] [$_S$ t_i saw t_j]]]

Note now that the subject t_i will be properly governed in (91) but not in (90) since $\overline{\text{S}}$, a maximal projection, intervenes between *who* and the variable t_i.

The analysis concerning the LF adjunction of a *wh*-element to $\overline{\text{S}}$-marked [+wh] has a number of consequences. In Aoun, Hornstein, and Sportiche 1981 the *[that-t]* effect is accounted for without reference to the notion of c-command. The authors assume the existence of the following general rule that applies at S-structure:

(92)

COMP Indexing

$[_{\text{COMP}} \overline{\overline{X}}_i...] \rightarrow [_{\text{COMP}_i} \overline{\overline{X}}_i...]$

iff COMP dominates only *i*-indexed elements.

This rule will correctly rule out (89) (**who do you think* $[_{\overline{S}} t_i$ *that* $[t_i$ *saw Bill]]*) since the presence of *that* in COMP will prevent the application of COMP Indexing; the trace in subject position will not be properly governed. Note that in order for this analysis to distinguish between (88) and (89), it is necessary to stipulate that COMP Indexing applies no later than S-structure. If it applied at LF, the presence of *what* in COMP in (88) would prevent its application, and the sentence would incorrectly be excluded for the same reasons excluding (89). If, however, it is assumed that the LF-movement rule that raises the *wh*-quantifier adjoins this quantifier to $\overline{\text{S}}$-marked [+wh]—that is, if a representation such as (91) is assumed instead of (88)—we would not need to stipulate that the application of COMP Indexing is restricted to S-structure.

This approach has a number of consequences. H. Koopman (1982) indicates that in French, movement to COMP in LF (i.e., *Wh*-Raising) does not create proper government. Her proposal is based on the behavior of *quoi* 'what' in French. As noted by H.-G. Obenauer (1976), *quoi* cannot appear in the complementizer of a tensed clause (**quoi as-tu vu* 'what did you see'). Koopman accounts for this restriction by a filtering mechanism applying in the PF component. The reason is that *Wh*-Raising, which applies in LF, does not obey this restriction:

(93)

a. tu   as vu quoi $\xrightarrow{\text{by } Wh\text{-Raising}}$

   you saw   what

b. $[_{\overline{S}}[_{\text{COMP}} \text{quoi}_i]$ [tu   as vu x_i]]

       what   you saw

   'what did you see'

A derivation such as (93a–b) is possible in French because the syntactic *Wh*-Movement is optional. If a *wh*-element has not been moved in Syntax, it will be raised in LF (Aoun, Hornstein, and Sportiche 1981). Now consider the following derivation discussed by Koopman:

(94)

a. $[\bar{s}[_{COMP}] [_{S}$ quoi est arrivé$]]$ $\xrightarrow{\text{ by } Wh\text{-Raising}}$

b. $*[\bar{s}[_{COMP}$ quoi$_i] [_{S} e_i$ est arrivé$]]$
    what   has arrived

Unlike (93b), (94b) is ungrammatical. As Koopman argues, this contrast may be accounted for if it is assumed that COMP Indexing applies no later than S-structure. In that case, the variable in (93b) will be properly governed by the verb. The variable in (94b) will be left non–properly governed, thus violating the ECP. Koopman concludes that since COMP Indexing applies no later than S-structure, movement to COMP in LF does not create proper government.

Assuming that COMP Indexing applies in LF, the insights of Koopman's analysis may be captured if *Wh*-Raising adjoins the *wh*-quantifier to S̄-marked [+wh] rather than to COMP (as in (90) and (91)). In that case the LF representation of (94a) after the application of *Wh*-Raising will be (95) and not (94b):

(95)

$*[_{\bar{s}}$ quoi$_i$ $[_{\bar{s}}[_{COMP}] [e_i$ est arrivé$]]]$

(95) will be ruled out for the same reason as (90): the *wh*-element fails to properly govern the empty element.

I have suggested that *Wh*-Raising adjoins the *wh*-quantifier to S̄-marked [+wh]. In particular, this has allowed us to account for the Superiority Condition by the ECP. We will return to the Superiority Condition in a somewhat different framework using some of the suggestions mentioned in this section. It is to be noted that if COMP Indexing provides the correct analysis, we will not need to refer to the notion of c-command to account for the *[*that-t*] effect.

2.8 Elimination of the Empty Category Principle for Variables

I turn now to the possibility of eliminating the redundancy that exists between the ECP and the generalized binding principles, both of which account for the *[*that-t*] effect found with variables. In this section I will indicate that the binding principles suffice to exclude these con-structures, thus eliminating the need for the ECP. As for NP-traces, some independent condition applying on the chain of coindexed elements will account for the cases covered by the ECP; I will discuss this condition in the sections to follow.

For variables, the core cases covered by the ECP are those illustrated in (76), repeated here:

(96)
a. *who$_i$ do you wonder [$_{\bar{S}}$ how [$_S$ t_i solved the problem]]
b. *who$_i$ do you think [$_{\bar{S}}$ t_i that [$_S$ t_i saw Bill]]
c. *it is unclear [$_{\bar{S}}$ what [$_S$ who saw t]]

These ungrammatical examples are ruled out by the binding principles. In the indirect question and *[*that-t*] cases, (96a) and (96b), the embedded $\bar{S}$ counts as the governing category for the variable in argument position; it contains a governor INFL (AGR) and an accessible SUBJECT (AGR):

(97)
a. *who$_i$ do you wonder [$_{\bar{S}}$* how [t_i [$_{INFL}$ AGR] solved the problem]]
b. *who$_i$ do you think [$_{\bar{S}}$* t_i that [$_S$ t_i saw Bill]]

In neither construction is the variable $\bar{A}$-bound in its governing category: in (96a) there is no potential $\bar{A}$-binder if it is assumed that there is no intermediate trace in COMP. If it is assumed that there is an intermediate trace in COMP, however, then (96a) reduces to (96b). In (96b) the structural description of COMP Indexing is not satisfied. The embedded COMP will not be coindexed with the empty category in subject position. As such, it will not $\bar{A}$-bind this empty category. (96a–b) are thus excluded by binding principle (A), which requires a variable to be $\bar{A}$-bound in its governing category.

As for the superiority case, (96c), we have assumed that the movement rule that raises the *wh*-element in argument position adjoins this quantifier to $\bar{S}$-marked [+wh] rather than to COMP, as in (98) (= (87)):

(98)
it is unclear [$_{\bar{S}}$ who$_i$ [$_{\bar{S}_0}$ what$_j$ [t_i saw t_j]]]

Moreover, to distinguish between (98) and (99) (= (88)), we indicated that $\bar{S}_0$, a maximal projection, blocks proper government of t_i:

(99)
it is unclear [$_{\bar{S}}$ what$_j$ [$_{\bar{S}_0}$ who$_i$ [t_i saw t_j]]]

Note that in (98) and (99) the minimal $\bar{S}$ containing a governor (INFL (AGR)) and an accessible SUBJECT (AGR) for t_i is $\bar{S}_0$. Only the variable t_i of (99) is $\bar{A}$-bound in this category; (98) will thus be excluded by the binding principles.

For variables, then, the core cases excluded by the ECP may be accounted for by the generalized binding principles. I now turn to more complex cases involving extraction of subjects from postverbal position in Italian.

2.8.1 Extraction of Subjects in Italian

Briefly, the argument of this section is as follows: In embedded structures in Italian, the postverbal, but not the preverbal, subject may be questioned. The nonextractability of an element in preverbal subject position is not surprising. It illustrates the well-known phenomenon of the *[that-t] effect, although the situation is complicated by the existence of an affix-movement rule applying in Syntax in Italian. The postverbal subject element may be extracted, however, since Affix-Movement cliticizes the AGR element to V; being in an $\bar{A}$-position, AGR will be able to $\bar{A}$-bind the variable left by the extraction rule. This analysis thus replaces the ECP account of Rizzi 1982a and LGB, where it is assumed that the V properly governs the postverbal subject position: $[_{\bar{S}} ...[_{VP}[_{VP} V + AGR] NP]]$.

Unlike English, Italian allows phonetically null subjects in tensed clauses (Rizzi 1982a):

(100)
a. verrà
b. *will come

(101)
a. verrà Gianni
b. *will come Gianni

(102)
a. chi$_i$ credi che t_i verrà
b. *who$_i$ do you think that t_i will come

Assuming the existence of a non–properly governed empty element in subject position, the ungrammaticality of the (b) examples is accounted for by the ECP. The grammaticality of the (a) examples illustrates the fact that the ECP does not seem to hold in languages allowing null subjects (PRO-drop languages).

The conclusion that the ECP appears to be void for Italian faces a number of problems. As L. Rizzi (1982a) points out, the *[*that-t*] effect—accounted for by the ECP—holds in Italian in spite of prima facie evidence to the contrary. Consider the following examples:

(103)

a. non voglio che tu   parli   con   nessuno
    I neg want that you speak with nobody

b. *non voglio che nessuno venga
    I neg want that nobody comes

c. voglio che nessuno venga
    I want that nobody comes

The corresponding LF representations are as follows:

(104)

a. [for no x], I want that you speak with x
b. [for no x], I want that x comes
c. I want that [for no x], x comes

Irrelevantly, (103b) may have the reading 'not (I want that for no x, x comes)'. The LF representations are derived on the assumptions in (105), following an analysis put forward by R. S. Kayne (1981c) and generalized to Italian by L. Rizzi (1982a) and to Spanish by O. Jaeggli (1982):

(105)

a. The particle *ne* is a scope operator, determining the scope of *nessuno*.
b. *Nessuno* undergoes Quantifier-Movement in the LF component.

The ungrammatical example (103b) illustrates a *[*that-t*] effect and thus falls under the ECP. It appears, then, that the ECP holds for variables formed by rules of the LF component in Italian but not for variables left by *Wh*-Movement. A solution to this problem is indicated by Rizzi, who points out that a fourth option is available in Italian in addition to (103a–c), namely (106):

(106)

non voglio che venga nessuno
[for no x], I want that comes x

Thus, although (103b) is barred, its sense can be expressed by (106), in which the subject follows the verb. (106) does not violate the ECP any more than (103a) does. In other words, PRO-drop languages actually observe the ECP, exactly as the non-PRO-drop languages do. The apparent examples to the contrary illustrated in (101a) are spurious; what in fact is happening is that movement in these cases takes place not from the subject position but from the postverbal position, in which the subject in PRO-drop languages may appear by virtue of a process of free inversion. Specifically, *Wh*-Movement of the subject in PRO-drop languages, which appears to violate the *[*that-t*] Filter (as in (102a)) actually takes place from the postverbal position, which is properly governed by V, rather than from the subject position, and, contrary to appearances, *Wh*-Movement does observe the *[*that-t*] Filter in Italian. The underlying structure for (107), then, is (108) rather than (109) (irrelevant details omitted):

(107)
chi credi che verrà
'who do you think that will come'

(108)
credi [$_{\bar{S}}$ che [$_S$ α verrà chi]]

(109)
credi [$_{\bar{S}}$ che [$_S$ chi verrà]]

It now follows that there is no contradiction between the apparent violation of the *[*that-t*] Filter in the PRO-drop languages and the assumption that the ECP (from which the filter derives) holds of variables quite generally, as a property of LF representations.

Before illustrating how the binding theory accounts for cases of postverbal subject extraction, as evidence that the cases accounted for by the ECP can be treated by the generalized binding theory, we must study the "inverted structure" more carefully:

(110)
α V NP

(111)
verrà Gianni
'Gianni will come'

Partially adopting the analysis suggested in LGB (section 4.5), we will assume that there is a rule of Affix-Movement that adjoins the elements of INFL to the initial verbal element of VP. As a consequence of the application of this rule, the postverbal subject will still be governed by

INFL—or more precisely by AGR—and will receive its nominative Case by virtue of being governed by AGR. The exact characterization of α in (110) is irrelevant for our discussion. In LGB it is taken to be a phonetically unrealized anaphoric pronominal (= PRO). In Chomsky 1982 it is taken to be a phonetically unrealized nonanaphoric pronominal (= pro). Whatever the exact characterization of this empty element, it is partially independent from the existence of Affix-Movement. That is, this rule is compatible either with the characterization of α given in LGB or with the one given in Chomsky 1982.

With this in mind, we can return to the contrast between a representation such as (104b) (= (112)) and (106) (= (113)):

(112)
*Q_i ... [$_{\bar{S}}$ che [$_S$ x_i V ...]]

(113)
Q_i ... [$_{\bar{S}}$ che [$_S$[$_{VP}$[$_{VP}$ V ...] x_i]]]

These examples show that in Italian, long extraction of the embedded subject is possible from the postverbal position only. In the GB framework the contrast between (112) and (113) is accounted for by the ECP. In (112) the variable is not properly governed, and the sentence is ruled out. However, (113) does not violate the ECP, since the postverbal empty category is properly governed by V (see Rizzi 1982a). It thus appears that the extraction of postverbal subjects in Italian is elegantly accounted for if the existence of a principle such as the ECP is assumed. As we shall see, however, the contrast between (112) and (113) can be accounted for without the ECP, by appealing to the generalized binding principles.

Let us first consider (113). Affix-Movement may apply in Syntax. The postverbal subject will be governed and Case-marked by AGR:

(114)
Q_i ... [$_{\bar{S}}$ che [[$_{VP}$[$_{VP}$ V + AGR] x_i]]]

As a result of applying this rule, AGR, which is in INFL, is attached to the head of V of VP—or, to present the matter differently, the effect of Affix-Movement is to *cliticize* AGR to V. Recalling that clitics are in $\bar{A}$-position and $\bar{A}$-bind a variable, consider the derived structure (114). The variable in postverbal subject position is in the c-command domain of AGR, which thus counts as a governor and an accessible SUBJECT. The minimal category containing AGR is the embedded clause. In this category, the variable is $\overline{A}$-bound by AGR, thus satisfying the binding principles.

In other words, (114) is treated like the Hebrew examples discussed in section 2.6.1, where the clitic $\overline{A}$-binds the variable left by the extraction of a *wh*-element from inside an NP:

(115)
$Q_i \ldots [_{NP} N + cl_i \ x_i]$

Note that this account correctly excludes A-anaphors such as reflexives and reciprocals from the postverbal subject position, since they will be A-free in their governing category, the embedded clause. In brief, Affix-Movement cliticizes the AGR element onto the verb V. Being like all clitics in nonargument position, this element will $\overline{A}$-bind the variable left in postverbal subject position by the extraction rules. When attached to V, AGR counts as a governor, an accessible SUBJECT, and an $\overline{A}$-binder. This accounts for (113).

This explanation for the lack of *[*that-t*] effect for a variable in postverbal subject position relies on the existence of Affix-Movement. In Aoun (to appear) I present a somewhat different account that does not rely on the existence of this rule. There, I suggest that AGR cannot count as an accessible SUBJECT for a variable in postverbal subject position. This variable thus will behave like a variable in object position with respect to the binding theory: neither variable will have an accessible SUBJECT. The root clause will be the domain in which the variables should be bound; hence the lack of a *[*that-t*] effect.

Regarding the ungrammaticality of (112) ($*Q_i \ldots [_{\bar{S}} che [_S x_i V \ldots]]$), two derivations are to be considered. In the first, Affix-Movement applies; in the second, it does not:

(116)
a. $*Q_i \ldots [_{\bar{S}} che [_S x_i [_{VP} V \ AGR]]]$
b. $*Q_i \ldots [_{\bar{S}} che [_S x_i \ AGR \ VP]]$

In section 2.6.1 we distinguished between three types of positions: A-positions, $\overline{A}$-positions, and head-positions. We also adopted the analysis according to which clitics are in $\overline{A}$-positions and may function as $\overline{A}$-binders, and stated that AGR, which is in INFL, is neither in an A-position nor in an $\overline{A}$-position, but rather in head-position. This is why in configurations where Affix-Movement did not apply, as in (116b), AGR neither A-binds nor $\overline{A}$-binds the subject position. With this in mind, let us consider (116b). Here, the minimal category containing a governor (AGR) and an accessible SUBJECT (AGR) for the variable is the embedded clause. In this governing category, the variable is $\overline{\text{A}}$-free and the derivation is ruled out by the binding principles. This illustrates the standard case of *[*that-t*] effect. In (116a), where Affix-Movement did apply in Syntax, the empty element x is not governed. Assuming that nominative Case, like other Case rules, is assigned or checked under government after the application of Affix-Movement, as suggested in LGB, the derivation will be excluded by the θ-Criterion under the Visibility Convention. (An empty element is taken to be "invisible" to rules of the LF component unless it is either PRO or Case-marked: [$_{NP}$ e] is invisible when it contains no Case.) If so, then no θ-role will be assigned to the invisible trace in (116a), or one will be assigned but will be invisible in LF, where the θ-Criterion is presumably checked (see LGB (chapter 5) and Aoun 1979). Consequently, the θ-Criterion, which requires every θ-role to be assigned to an argument, will be violated. Thus, (116a) will be excluded for the same reason as (117):

(117)
who did you try [t to win]

In (117), which is discussed in LGB, the trace is not Case-marked and cannot bear the θ-role assigned by the VP *to win;* the sentence will be ruled out by the θ-Criterion. Note that any GB theory treatment of (116a) may be applied; the analysis of this construction does not involve any proposal specific to the approach outlined here.

2.8.2 Two Notions of C-Command

Recalling that the above analysis replaces the ECP account that assumes that V properly governs the postverbal subject position,

(118)
[$_{\bar{S}}$ ... [$_{VP}$[$_{VP}$ V + AGR] NP]]

let us now consider sentences containing this position in more detail. We find such examples as (119a–b):

(119)
a. telefonato molti studenti
   telephone many students
   'many students telephone'

b. arrivano molti studenti
   arrive   many students
   'many students arrive'

There is evidence that the two cases differ in structure. Case (119a) has the adjoined structure (120a); case (119b), the VP-internal structure (120b):

(120)
a. [$_{VP}$[$_{VP}$ telefonato] [$_{NP}$ molti studenti]]
b. [$_{VP}$ arrivano [$_{NP}$ molti studenti]]

Supporting this conclusion is the fact that *ne*-cliticization is possible in (119b) but not in (119a), giving (121a–b):

(121)
a. *ne   telefonato molti
   of-them telephone many

b. ne   arrivano molti
   of-them arrive   many

Let us assume that the relation between *ne* and its trace is essentially an antecedent-anaphor relation. As an antecedent, *ne* must c-command its trace; (121a) is therefore ungrammatical because *ne* does not c-command the trace it is coindexed with. L. Burzio (1981) presents evidence supporting the difference between (120a) and (120b) and the further conclusion that in (119a) a rule of inversion from subject position has applied—an adjunction rule, adjoining the subject *molti studenti* (or *molti ne*) to the VP—whereas in (119b) the subject *molti studenti* (or *molti ne*) is base-generated in the object position of the VP (also see Belletti and Rizzi 1981).

Assuming that this analysis is correct, these constructions refer to two notions of c-command: the first allows the V—or in our terms the AGR element cliticized onto the verb—to c-command the postverbal subject position in (120a); the second, defined in (122), prevents *ne*-cliticization from the postverbal subject position in (120a):

(122)
α c-commands β iff every maximal projection dominating α dominates β, and $\alpha \neq \beta$.
(Cf. Aoun and Sportiche 1983.)

One may hope to dispense with this distinction, which is pointed out in LGB (p. 166). To achieve this, some general remarks concerning feature assignment will be necessary. In Aoun 1981a I remarked on the parallelism between case assignment and "mood assignment." Standard Arabic, for instance, exhibits two types of complementizers appearing with completive clauses. The occurrence of each of these complementizers depends on the choice of the matrix verb: *believe*-type verbs (*ʔaʕtaqidu, ʔaðunnu*, etc.) require *ʔanna*, and *want*-type verbs (*ʔawaddu, ʔuri:du*, etc.) *ʔan*.

ʔanna is a case-assigning element and *ʔan* a mood-assigning element; they assign accusative and subjunctive (*muḍa:riʕ manṣu:b*), respectively:

(123)

a. ʔanna
    [+acc]
b. ʔan
    [+subj]

The accusative and subjunctive features generated with the complementizers will be paired with a lexical NP and a verb, respectively. As usual, this pairing requires adjacency (Vergnaud (forthcoming), Aoun 1979, Stowell 1981). It follows that *ʔanna* is followed by a lexical NP and *ʔan* by a verb:

(124)

a. ʔanna NP → ʔanna   NP
    [+acc]   [+acc]
b. ʔan V → ʔan   V
    [+subj]   [+subj]

It is tempting to collapse the two features into one: [±mood], for instance. [+mood] will be interpreted as subjunctive and [−mood] as accusative. Or, to put things in a slightly different way, it is possible to suppose that there is one complementizer for completive sentences,

(125)

COMP
[±mood]

and that the matrix verb selects the feature [+mood] or [−mood]. When [+mood] is selected, the complementizer is realized as *ʔan;* when [−mood] is selected, the complementizer is realized as *ʔanna.* The situation is somewhat similar in English, where *that* appears with a tensed clause and *for* with a nontensed clause; the latter, but not the former, is assumed to assign Case. Note also that the same formal mechanism (namely, government) is used in Standard Arabic for Case and mood assignment: the complementizer governs the element to which it assigns a feature (Rouveret 1980).

Let us try to generalize these remarks and consider that verbs receive mood via government, trying also to keep the parallelism between Case and mood assignment as close as possible.

The Case-feature is assigned by a governor X^0 to a governed nominal element $\overline{\overline{X}}$:

(126)

This Case-feature percolates down (or is copied) onto the head of $\overline{\overline{X}}$:

(127)

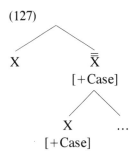

Let us assume the same mechanism for mood assignment: INFL may be viewed as the governor assigning mood to VP; this mood will percolate down (or will be copied) onto the head V:

(128)

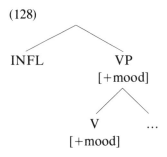

The similarity between (128) and Affix-Movement is obvious: both the mood-feature and INFL end up being attached to V. Let us tentatively assume that they are the same and that (128) illustrates the application of Affix-Movement. In other words, Affix-Movement proceeds in two steps: first INFL is attached to VP, and then it percolates down (or is copied onto) the head V. Percolation down to the head may presumably be viewed as a PF phenomenon. (The status of the empty element left by Affix-Movement is discussed in LGB, section 4.5; it is irrelevant for the purpose of our discussion.) Structures (129a–c) illustrate this process:

(129)

a.

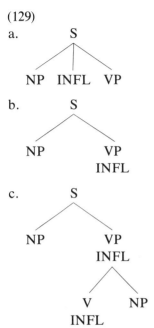

This method of applying Affix-Movement may help dispense with the distinction between two types of c-command. Let us assume the existence of the more restricted notion only, given in (122). INFL (or more precisely AGR in (118)) is able to c-command the postverbal subject, since it is first attached to VP. However, the head V of VP will not c-command this NP. Consequently, AGR may serve as an accessible SUBJECT for the NP, as a governor assigning Case to this NP, and as an $\bar{\text{A}}$-binder for the empty element left by the extraction of this NP, but *ne*-cliticization, which adjoins the clitic *ne* to V, will create a structure where the trace is not c-commanded by *ne*. The result will thus be filtered out under the assumption that *ne* must c-command its trace.

Being attached (or more precisely adjoined) to VP in the course of Affix-Movement, AGR will c-command the postverbal subject NP; it will thus count as an accessible SUBJECT for this NP. Being cliticized and coindexed with this NP, it will also count as an $\bar{\text{A}}$-binder of this NP. However, as pointed out by L. Rizzi (personal communication), (118) contains two VPs. If INFL is attached to the higher one, AGR (which is contained in INFL) will dominate the postverbal subject and thus will not count as an accessible SUBJECT, a governor, or an Ā-binder. In short, we must assume that INFL is attached to the lower VP. Note that if INFL does not govern the postverbal subject, this subject will not receive Case and the derivation will be filtered out by the Case Filter. We are assuming that Case assignment applies in a context of government (cf. section 2.3.1) and that Case is not transmitted from the preverbal subject position as suggested in Safir 1982. To obtain this result, many possibilities come to mind. The simplest is to assume that INFL randomly attaches to either of the two VPs. There will thus be a grammatical derivation—namely, the one where INFL attaches to the lower VP. This is the required result.

Another question with respect to these constructions is the following: since AGR may count as an Ā-binder for the empty element left by the extraction of the postverbal subject, why does it not count as an Ā-binder for the empty element left by the cliticization of *ne* from inside this subject? Recall that for an empty element to bind another element, it must c-command this element and be coindexed with it. INFL (AGR) is coindexed with the subject NP and c-commands it; thus, it may count as a binder of this subject. However, it may not bind an empty element contained in this subject because it is not coindexed with this empty element. Furthermore, AGR *cannot* be coindexed with this empty element because it would be coindexed with the subject and with an empty element contained in this subject, thus violating the *i*-within-*i* Condition:

(130)
$AGR_p \ldots [_{NP_p} \ldots e_p]$

This incidentally indicates that AGR does not count as an accessible SUBJECT for the empty element left by *ne*-cliticization from a postverbal subject position. Assuming that *ne* must c-command its trace, it is possible to derive the c-command requirement from the binding principles. Note, however, that AGR will not count as an accessible SUBJECT; it remains to be seen whether this empty element is governed.

Like French *en* (Kayne 1975), Italian *ne* corresponds to a genitival noun. Assuming that Case assignment is a special case of government, this means that the genitival noun that corresponds to *ne* received its Case by virtue of being governed in the phrase in which it occurs. Assuming also that the trace left by the cliticization of the genitival noun from the subject position is governed, the root clause will count as a governing category for this empty element, since it lacks an accessible SUBJECT (in a simplex sentence such as (118), for instance). The derivation will be ruled out by the binding theory, since in the root clause the empty element will be free.

Now consider the following representation, where the embedded INFL is attached to the embedded VP (irrelevant details omitted):

(131)

NP AGR V + ne$_i$ [$_S$ ... [$_{VP}$ VP [$_{NP}$ molti t_i]]]
              [+INFL]

The embedded AGR in INFL cannot count as a SUBJECT accessible to the trace, since it is coindexed with the NP containing this trace. The first accessible SUBJECT is therefore the matrix AGR, and the governing category is the matrix clause. In this category the empty element is bound by *ne*. We therefore expect (131) to be grammatical; but this is not the case.

In section 4.4 I will argue that for an element X to cliticize onto an element Y, two conditions must be met. The first concerns the binding theory: the relation between the clitic and the empty element it is coindexed with must not violate the binding theory. The second concerns the relationship between X and Y: for X to be cliticized onto Y, X must be a dependent of Y. Roughly for the purpose of this discussion, "X is a dependent of Y" is equivalent to "X is governed by Y." In (131) the binding principles are not violated. The second requirement is, however, since the matrix verb does not govern the position from which *ne* has been cliticized. Note that when *ne* is extracted from inside an object NP, no violation occurs:

(132)

[$_{VP}$ V + ne$_i$ [$_{NP}$ molti t_i]]

In (132) the V governs the NP. Assuming as in Belletti and Rizzi 1981 that whenever an NP is governed by X the head of this NP is governed by X and that the position occupied by the empty element in (132) is the head of NP, the position from which *ne* has been cliticized will be governed by (a dependent of) the V. Hence, cliticization is possible.

We have thus accomplished our purpose of dispensing with the need for two notions of c-command by exploiting the similarity between Case and mood assignment.

2.8.3 Preposition Stranding and Empty QPs

Another problem accounted for by the ECP involves preposition stranding (Van Riemsdijk 1978, Hornstein and Weinberg 1981):

(133)

who did John speak to x_i

(134)

*qui_i Jean a parlé avec x_i

As indicated in LGB (section 5.1), if it is assumed that prepositions are not proper governors, preposition stranding will be excluded in general by the ECP since the empty category left behind will not be properly governed. It will be permitted only in case a marked rule allows proper government by V: a rule that in effect permits the preposition to "transmit" proper government from the verbal head (Kayne 1981b). English but not French displays this marked option; consequently, preposition stranding is allowed in the former language but not in the latter.

In a framework that dispenses with the ECP, this proposal cannot be maintained. There is, however, some evidence suggesting that preposition stranding is not to be accounted for by the ECP. Consider the following contrast in French:

(135)

a. *Jean veut   que qui vienne
   Jean wants that who come
   'who does Jean want to come'

b. Jean veut   que Marie voit qui
    Jean wants that Marie see who
    'who does Jean want Marie to see'

Extending the analysis suggested in Kayne 1981c to French, it is indicated in Aoun, Hornstein, and Sportiche 1981 that the contrast between (135a) and (135b) may be accounted for by the ECP if it is assumed—following Chomsky 1973—that Move α in LF raises the *wh*-quantifier to the matrix COMP:

(136)

a. *qui_i Jean veut que x_i vienne
b. qui_i Jean veut que Marie voit x_i

In (136b), but not in (136a), the variable is properly governed by V: (136a) will be ruled out by the ECP.

Now consider the following sentence:

(137)
Jean veut   que [$_{NP}$ le   portrait de qui] soit vendu
Jean wants that   the portrait of who be   sold
'whose portrait does Jean want to be sold'

The grammaticality of (137) indicates that there is no pied-piping in LF. To see why, consider the representation where the whole NP has been pied-piped in LF and the one where it has not:

(138)
a. [le portrait de qui]$_i$ Jean veut que x_i soit vendu
b. $\langle_a$ de$\rangle$ qui$_i$ Jean veut que [$_{NP}$ le portrait $\langle_b$ de$\rangle$ x_i soit vendu
   Either a or b.

In (138a), where the whole NP has been pied-piped, the variable is left in non–properly governed position like the one in (136a); the derivation should be ruled out by the ECP. The grammaticality of (137) leads us to choose the LF representation (138b), where the variable is presumably properly governed or, in our terms, $\overline{\text{A}}$-bound by the prenominal position, as argued in section 2.4.

To be more precise, the discussion of (137) is also compatible with the assumption that pied-piping is optional in LF. The following facts, however, indicate that this is not the case and that a stronger conclusion—that there is no pied-piping in LF—should be adopted. Consider the following sentences (cf. LGB and Aoun, Sportiche, Vergnaud, and Zubizarreta 1980):

(139)
a. quels livres que Jean$_i$ a lus a-t-il$_i$ aimé
    'which books that Jean read did he like'
b. *il$_i$ a aimé quels livres que Jean$_i$ a lus
    'he liked which books that Jean read'

In (139a), where the phrase containing the *wh*-element has been moved in Syntax, coreference between *Jean* and *il* is possible. In (139b) the phrase containing the *wh*-element has not been moved in Syntax (syntactic *Wh*-Movement being optional in French (Aoun, Hornstein, and Sportiche 1981), and intended coreference between *il* and *Jean* is impossible. This is accounted for if pied-piping does not apply at LF. As stated in section 2.6, the binding theory must apply at LF, and I will argue in chapter 3 that it must apply at S-structure as well. With this in mind, consider (139b). We are adopting the standard assumption concerning indexing; namely, that indexing between two elements may freely apply at S-structure or at LF. (We will reconsider this assumption in chapter 3.) If at S-structure we choose to coindex *il* and *Jean*, binding principle (C) will be violated. If, however, we choose to apply free indexing not at S-structure but at LF, the representation will be well-formed at S-structure but not at LF under the assumption that pied-piping does not apply at LF. Suppose that pied-piping were optional at LF. Then two LF representations would be available for (139b), one in which the whole phrase containing the *wh*-element has been fronted by Move α in LF (derivation 1) and one in which only the *wh*-element has been fronted (derivation 2). The output of derivation 1 will essentially be similar to (139a). In other words, if optional pied-piping in LF were assumed, there would incorrectly be a derivation allowing *il* and *Jean* in (139b) to be coreferential. If, however, it is assumed that there is no pied-piping in LF, the contrast between (139a) and (139b) will be correctly accounted for: in (139b)—but not in (139a)—coindexing of *il* and *Jean* will violate binding principle (C), since a name *Jean* will be A-bound by *il* (or more precisely by the empty element left by the clitic in subject position).

Having established that there is no pied-piping in LF, let us consider the following sentence:

(140)
Jean a parlé avec qui
Jean spoke   with who
'who did Jean speak to'

Assuming the nonexistence of pied-piping in LF, the LF representation of (140) will be (141):

(141)
qui$_i$ Jean a parlé avec x_i

In (141) the variable generated by an LF movement rule is left in non–properly governed position. The derivation must be ruled out by the ECP, which applies in LF. However, (140) is grammatical.

In other words, (140), where the *wh*-element has been left in its base-generated position, has exactly the same LF representation as (134), where syntactic *Wh*-Movement has applied. (140) is grammatical, but (134) is not. The ECP, which applies in LF, will not distinguish between the two sentences: it will mark both sentences ungrammatical if it is assumed that prepositions are not proper governors or will mark both of them grammatical if it is assumed that prepositions are proper governors. Whatever option is chosen, it is clear that the ECP cannot account for the phenomenon of preposition stranding: since (134) and (140) essentially have similar LF representations, an LF principle such as the ECP will not be able to distinguish between them. In PF, however, (134) and (140) will have distinct representations. This may be taken to suggest that preposition stranding is to be accounted for by a PF filter, presumably along the lines of Hornstein and Weinberg 1981. Basing himself on different facts, C.-T. J. Huang (1982) reaches similar conclusions concerning the nonexistence of pied-piping in LF. In section 3.7 we will reconsider this conclusion.

Another phenomenon accounted for by the ECP concerns NPs of the form *de N* . . . in French. In certain negative environments, French permits objects of the form *de N* . . . (the following discussion is based on work by R. S. Kayne (1981b)):

(142)
a. Jean n'a pas trouvé   de   livres
   Jean (neg) has not found (of) books
   'Jean has not found any books'

b. *Jean a trouvé de livres

Kayne (1975) suggests that these NPs may be analyzed as in (143),

(143)
[$_{NP}$ zero element–de–articleless NP]

the idea being that (142a) is entirely comparable to (144), except that where (144) contains *beaucoup* 'many', (142a) contains a zero element of the same category:

(144)
Jean n'a pas trouvé   beaucoup de   livres
Jean (neg) has not found many   (of) books

As Kayne indicates (1981b), there is a clear advantage to considering the zero element of (142a) as an instance of an empty category—an empty QP—subject to the ECP. This move straightforwardly accounts for the asymmetry between (142a) and (145a–b):

(145)

a. *de livres n'ont   pas été   trouvés (par Jean)
   (of) books (neg) have not been found   (by Jean)

b. *de gâteaux ne   me déplairaient   pas
   (of) cakes   (neg) me would displease not

The fact that [$_{NP}$[$_{QP}$ e] de . . .] is not permitted in surface subject position follows from the ECP, since in such positions QP is not properly governed. Similarly, the ECP accounts for the asymmetry between (146a) and (146b) and for the ungrammaticality of (147a–b):

(146)

a. Jean ne voudrait pas   que tu   boives de bière
   Jean (neg) would not like that you drink   (of) beer

b. *Jean ne voudrait pas   que de bière lui coule dessus
   Jean (neg) would not like that (of) beer spill on him

(147)

a. *Jean n'a pas parlé   à de linguistes
   Jean (neg) has not spoken to (of) linguists

b. *Jean n'a pas voté   pour de communistes
   Jean (neg) has not voted for (of) Communists

Once again, by excluding prepositions from the set of proper governors the ECP can be invoked to account for (147a–b) (see Kayne 1981b for further details). Nonetheless, some restrictions are needed with respect to the conclusion that the ECP accounts for the ungrammaticality of these sentences. These restrictions may be traced back to our earlier discussion of preposition stranding and to the following facts concerning *ne . . . personne*. The discussion of *ne . . . nessuno* in Italian in section 2.8.1 was a generalization of Kayne's (1981c) analysis of *ne . . . personne*. Recall that it was assumed that

(148)

a. The particle *ne* is a scope operator, determining the scope of *nessuno (personne)*.

b. *Nessuno (personne)* undergoes Quantifier-Movement rule in the LF component.

These assumptions permit an ECP account of the following contrast (see Kayne 1981c):

(149)

a. ?je n'exige   que tu   vois personne
   I (neg) require that you see nobody

b. *je n'exige   que personne vienne
   I (neg) require that nobody   comes

Assuming (148a–b), the LF representations of (149a–b) are (150a–b):

(150)

a. [for no x] I require that you see x
b. [for no x] I require that x comes

As indicated for the Italian examples in section 2.8.1, the ungrammatical example (149b) illustrates a *[*that-t*] effect and thus falls under the ECP. Now consider (151a) and its LF representation (151b):

(151)

a. ?je n'exige   que tu   parles avec personne
   I (neg) require that you speak with nobody

b. [for no x] I require that you speak with x

This LF representation is derived under assumptions (148a–b) and the assumption that there is no pied-piping in LF. In light of the proposal that prepositions are not proper governors, the grammaticality of (151a) comes as a surprise: since the variable is not properly governed in (151b), we should expect the derivation to be excluded in the same way as (147a–b). The situation is therefore similar to the one concerning preposition stranding. The ECP, which applies in LF, will not distinguish between (147a–b) on the one hand and (151a) on the other: it will mark all three sentences ungrammatical if it is assumed that prepositions are not proper governors or will mark them all grammatical if it is assumed that prepositions are proper governors.

To summarize: It has been suggested that preposition stranding and QPs are accounted for by the ECP; consequently, any attempt to suggest that the cases covered by the ECP may be accounted for by the generalized binding principles must deal with these phenomena as well. However, we have seen that in fact these constructions cannot be accounted for by the ECP; since this principle applies in LF, it does not distinguish between the ungrammatical representations where the empty element is generated in Syntax either by Move α as in (133) or by the base rules as in (147a–b) and the grammatical representations where the empty element is generated by LF movement rules ((140)

and (151a)), since in LF both representations will be identical. On the other hand, for the reasons mentioned in LGB, Kayne 1981b, Rizzi 1982a, and Aoun, Hornstein, and Sportiche 1981, it cannot be suggested that the empty elements generated by LF rules are not subject to the ECP (cf. also the discussion of the *ne . . . nessuno* facts in section 2.8.1). Note, however, that any PF principle such as the one referred to above will distinguish between the ungrammatical and grammatical representations in question.

Despite all this, let us assume for the purpose of the discussion that preposition stranding is to be accounted for in terms of the ECP—in other words, that prepositions are not proper governors. In the framework that we are assuming, where the ECP is dispensed with, a governing category is the minimal category containing a governor and an accessible SUBJECT. A possibility in this framework will be to consider that the notion of accessible SUBJECT enters into the definition of governing categories only for those categories (NP, $\bar{S}$, etc.) that may have SUBJECTs. For NP and $\bar{S}$, two elements will be required for the definition of governing category: a governor and an accessible SUBJECT. For prepositions, only a governor will be required.

As expected, this proposal will have a number of consequences and will face a number of problems. For example, consider the following structure:

(152)
NP V [$_{PP}$ P anaphor]

Assuming the modification of the notion of governing category suggested above, PP will count as the governing category for the anaphor in (152). This virtually excludes anaphors inside PP. The facts are inconclusive; anaphors are sometimes allowed inside PPs and sometimes not:

(153)
a. John spoke to me about himself
b. Jean m'a parlé de lui

(154)
a. John always keeps his wits about him (*himself, *Bill)
b. the melody has a haunting character to it (*itself, *Bill)

(155)
a. John pushed the book away from him
b. John drew the book towards him
c. John turned his friends against him
d. John saw a snake near him

(156)
a. *they turned their friends against each other
b. they turned their arguments against each other

These examples are taken from LGB (pp. 289–290). As indicated there, in (154) a proximate pronoun is obligatory; in (155) it is optional. Judgments tend to waver about whether a proximate pronoun or an anaphor should be used in some of the examples of (155). Obscure factors enter into the decision: compare (155c) with (157):

(157)
John turned the argument against himself
(*him with *him* coreferential to *John*)

2.9 NP-Traces and the Empty Category Principle

Having accounted for the behavior of variables in terms of the generalized binding principles rather than the ECP, we now have a choice: whether to maintain the ECP for NP-traces or to try to dispense with it entirely. If achieved, the second approach would have the advantage of eliminating the redundancy that both the binding principles and the ECP require an antecedent for the trace left by NP-Movement: principle (A) of the binding theory requires the NP-trace (an anaphor) to have a c-commanding antecedent, and the ECP also requires a c-commanding antecedent (or a lexical governor). In this section and the next I argue that the second approach is correct.

The ECP is not restricted to variables left by the extraction of *wh*-elements. It also applies to traces left by the extraction of NPs, as in (158):

(158)
*John$_i$ is illegal [$_{\bar{S}}$[$_S$ t_i to leave]]

Representation (158) is ruled out by the ECP since the trace is left in non–properly governed position. Clearly, the binding principles are irrelevant in this instance: the trace does not have a governor, and since the embedded infinitival clause lacks AGR, the trace will not be governed in this clause. According to the definition of government adopted in section 2.3.1, $\overline{S}$ is an absolute barrier for government: the trace is not governed in the matrix clause either. Therefore, this empty category, which is an anaphor, does not have a governing category, and binding principle (A) will be inoperative.

The raising predicates of (159a–c) directly contrast with the predicate of (158):

(159)
a. John$_i$ is likely [t_i to be a nice fellow]
b. John$_i$ is certain [t_i to leave]
c. John$_i$ seems [t_i to be a nice fellow]

This contrast is accounted for by the ECP under the assumption that in (159a–c) the trace is properly governed. Given the definition of (proper) government, the sole candidate for proper governor in (159a–c) is the matrix predicate. Thus, in (159a–c), but not in (158), the trace is properly governed by the matrix predicate. Since $\overline{S}$ is a barrier for government, this amounts to saying that in (159a–c) $\overline{S}$ is "transparent": it allows proper government by the matrix predicate. This process of $\overline{S}$-transparency occurs after verbal or adjectival predicates such as those exemplified in (159a–c); it is this property that characterizes raising predicates. The process of $\overline{S}$-transparency is restricted to infinitival clauses. When an infinitival clause is not a complement of a raising predicate, the subject position of this complement will be ungoverned; only PRO may appear:

(160)
a. I persuaded Bill [PRO to leave]
b. I was sorry [PRO to leave]

In brief, in general the subject of an infinitival is PRO. A language such as English permits a marked exception after certain predicates that trigger a process of $\overline{S}$-transparency. This process allows the subject of the "transparent" clause to be properly governed by the matrix predicate. For concreteness, we will assume, as suggested in LGB, that this process rewrites $\overline{S}$ as S.

2.10 Elimination of the Empty Category Principle for NP-Traces

I would now like to suggest that the cases of NP-traces covered by the ECP may be accounted for by the θ-Criterion.

Consider the following sentence:

(161)
John hit the man

LF is so designed that such expressions as *John, the man* are assigned thematic roles (θ-roles). Thus, *John* in (161) bears the θ-role "agent" and *the man* the θ-role "patient." Expressions such as *John* and *the man* in (161), referred to as *arguments,* are distinct from such terms as the nonreferential *it* of (162a) or the existential *there* of (162b), which assume no θ-role:

(162)
a. it is certain that John will win
b. there are believed to be unicorns in the garden

NP arguments include names, variables, reflexives, reciprocals, clauses, and pronouns, and nonarguments include nonreferential expressions (*there,* impersonal pronominals, etc.).

The assignment of θ-roles to arguments is constrained by the well-formedness condition known as the θ-Criterion (see LGB, section 2.2 and chapter 5):

(163)
θ-Criterion
Each argument bears one and only one θ-role, and each θ-role is assigned to one and only one argument.

In (161) *John* and *the man* are in θ-positions; they will receive their θ-role by virtue of being in these positions. However, the subject position of a passive clause is not a θ-position, as indicated by the fact that a nonargument can appear in this position. In general, it follows from the Projection Principle advocated in LGB (section 2.2) that a nonargument cannot appear in a θ-position:

(164)
it was believed that John left

Note that an argument can appear in a non-θ-position:

(165)
the man$_i$ was hit t_i

When this happens, the argument receives its θ-role by virtue of being coindexed with the trace, which is in a θ-position; in (165) *the man* is interpreted as the "patient." More precisely, it is assumed that θ-roles are assigned to A-chains and that an argument receives its θ-role by virtue of being in an A-chain that contains an element in a θ-position. An A-chain may be informally characterized as follows:

(166)
a. NP-traces and their antecedents form an A-chain.
b. An NP in an A-position that is not coindexed with an NP-trace forms an A-chain by itself.

Thus, in (161) *John* and *the man* each form a chain, each of which is assigned a distinct θ-role. In (165) *the man* and the trace form a single chain, which is assigned a θ-role because the trace is in a θ-position.

With this in mind, let us return to our previous cases of NP-traces covered by the ECP:

(167)
a. *John$_i$ is illegal [$_{\bar{S}}$[$_S$ t_i to leave]]   (= (158))
b. John$_i$ is certain [$_S$ t_i to leave]   (= (159b))

The minimal difference between these two structures is that the latter involves a process of $\bar{S}$-Deletion or $\bar{S}$-Transparency. As a result, only the trace in (167b) will be properly governed, thus satisfying the ECP.

I would like to suggest that the primary function of this process is not to allow proper government of the embedded trace by the matrix verb. Rather, its primary function is to allow the antecedent of the trace—*John* in (167b)—and the trace to form a well-formed chain. Specifically, I suggest that $\bar{S}$ breaks an A-chain.

Given this assumption, the contrast between (167a) and (167b) may now be accounted for by the θ-Criterion. In these sentences the argument *John* appears in non-θ-position, as indicated by the fact that a nonreferential element such as *it* can appear in this position:

(168)
a. it is illegal for John to leave
b. it is certain that John will leave

A representation containing an argument in non-θ-position is well formed with respect to the θ-Criterion if the argument occurs in a chain to which a θ-role is assigned. Since $\bar{S}$ breaks an A-chain, there are two chains in (167a): one containing *John* and the other containing the trace. The former is assigned no θ-role, since *John* is not in a θ-position; the latter is assigned no θ-role either, since the trace is not Case-marked. Under the Visibility Convention discussed in section 2.8.1, an empty category may receive a θ-role if it is Case-marked—in terms of chains, if it is in a Case-marked chain—or if it is PRO. Thus, (167a) is excluded by the θ-Criterion: there is no θ-role assigned to the argument *John;* there is no argument to bear the θ-role assigned by the embedded predicate. In (167b), however, there is no θ-Criterion violation: *John* and the trace are in the same chain and *John* is Case-marked. Therefore, the embedded predicate will assign a θ-role to this chain.

Now consider examples (169a–c) and their S-structures (170a–c) (from LGB, p. 252):

(169)
a.   Bill was believed to have seen Tom
b.   *Bill was preferred (for) to have seen Tom
c.   *Bill was wanted to have seen Tom

(170)
a.   Bill$_i$ was believed [$_S$ t_i to have seen Tom]
b.   *Bill$_i$ was preferred [$_{\bar{S}}$ for [$_S$ t_i to have seen Tom]]
c.   *Bill$_i$ was wanted [$_{\bar{S}}$ for [$_S$ t_i to have seen Tom]]

In LGB the contrast between (170a) and (170b–c) is accounted for by the ECP: the embedded trace in (170a) is properly governed by the matrix verb, but *for* in (170b–c), like all prepositions, is not a proper governor.

If the ECP is dispensed with, the contrast between (170a) and (170b–c) may, once again, be accounted for by the θ-Criterion. In (170a), where $\bar{S}$-Deletion applies, *Bill* and the trace belong to the same chain, to which the embedded predicate assigns a θ-role. In (170b–c) $\bar{S}$-Deletion does not apply; *Bill* and its trace will be in separate chains. If it is assumed that *for* assigns Case, the chain containing the empty element will be Case-marked and thus will be able to receive a θ-role. However, the chain containing *Bill* will not receive a θ-role because it is not in a context of θ-assignment. Therefore, (170b–c) are ruled out by the θ-Criterion.

The proposal that $\bar{S}$ breaks an A-chain thus allows us to rule out cases of NP-traces left in non–properly governed positions by appealing to the θ-Criterion. The intuitive idea behind this proposal is that the proposition is the domain in which a chain may occur, where proposition is taken to be delimited by $\bar{S}$ rather than S.

There are sentences ruled out by the ECP that a priori do not seem to be accounted for by the θ-Criterion:

(171)
*there is unclear [$_{\bar{S}}$ how [$_S$ t_i to be a unicorn in the garden]]

In (171) *there* has been raised from a non–properly governed position: the representation is ruled out by the ECP. Neither *there* nor its trace is an argument or in a context of θ-assignment; the θ-Criterion therefore seems irrelevant. However, this conclusion is incorrect. In order to be assigned a θ-role, a chain must be Case-marked or headed by PRO. In LGB (chapter 6) it is assumed that *there* and the postverbal NP form a chain. If this analysis is correct, (171) will be ruled out by the θ-Criterion under the assumption that $\bar{S}$ breaks an A-chain. In (171) there will be two chains: the one containing *there* and the one containing the empty element and the postverbal NP (*t, a unicorn*). The latter chain is neither Case-marked nor headed by PRO; therefore, it will not receive a θ-role and the derivation will be ruled out by the θ-Criterion. This analysis crucially assumes that the postverbal NP receives its Case by virtue of being coindexed with *there* and not directly from the verb *to be*. This assumption is necessary if, as argued in LGB (chapter 6), the Case Filter (which requires NPs to be Case-marked) follows from the θ-Criterion and is not an independent principle in the grammar. Suppose that in (171) the postverbal NP were to receive its Case directly from the verb *to be*. We would incorrectly predict that (172) is grammatical, since the whole chain (*there, a unicorn*) would be Case-marked:

(172)
*it is unclear [$_{\bar{S}}$ how [$_S$ there to be a unicorn in the garden]]

Let us assume, nevertheless, that the θ-Criterion and the Case Filter are independent principles. (171) will still be ruled out under the assumption that $\bar{S}$ breaks an A-chain. In chapter 3 I will argue that in order to be interpreted, *there* must be lowered in LF to the same clause containing the NP with which it forms a chain—*a unicorn* in (171)—and that the domain of this lowering process is the chain. In (171), since $\bar{S}$ breaks an A-chain, the nonreferential *there* will not be lowered; thus, it will not be interpreted, and the sentence will be excluded. In brief, the assumption that $\bar{S}$ breaks an A-chain will account for all cases of NP-traces covered by the ECP.

2.10.1 Chains and Improper Movement
The assumption that $\bar{S}$ breaks an A-chain has two other advantages: the first concerns cases of improper movement, and the second concerns

the elimination of some redundancies involving the phonetically un-realized pronominal element.

The following derivation illustrates improper movement:

(173)

*John tried [$_{\bar{S}}$ t [t' to win]]

This derivation is discussed in LGB (section 3.2.3) and ruled out there under the assumption that an element in COMP breaks a chain, or more generally by restricting chains to elements in A-positions. The sentence is grammatical but not with the derivation indicated, where the matrix subject moves from the D-structure position of t' to the COMP position of t and then to the matrix position.

It can be shown that the θ-Criterion accounts for (173) under the assumption that $\bar{S}$ breaks an A-chain. In (173) *John* and the empty element are in two different chains. The chain containing *John* will not be assigned a θ-role since it is not in a context of θ-assignment. In fact, the θ-Criterion is violated a second time since the embedded predicate will not assign its θ-role to the subject position: the chain containing the trace is not Case-marked.

Now consider more complex derivations where improper movement occurs in a context of $\bar{S}$-Deletion (which was assumed to be a process rewriting $\bar{S}$ as S):

(174)

*John seems [$_S$ t [t' to have left]]

A derivation such as this will not be ruled out by the θ-Criterion unless it is assumed that the process of $\bar{S}$-Transparency or $\bar{S}$-Deletion is pre-vented from applying when COMP is filled by an overt or an empty element. Note that $\bar{S}$-Deletion is impossible in structures such as (175) where COMP is filled by an overt *wh*-element:

(175)

it is unclear [$_{\bar{S}}$ what to do]

Some consequences of this proposal are discussed in LGB (section 3.3.2).

2.10.2 Chains and PRO

Another advantage of the assumption that $\bar{S}$ breaks an A-chain is more technical in nature. It concerns the fact that the pronominal empty category, PRO, seems to occur as the head of a chain only. In LGB two principles single out PRO as the head of a chain: the Visibility Convention and the definition of chain (see LGB, chapter 5):

(176)
Visibility Convention
For a chain to receive a θ-role, it must be either Case-marked or headed by PRO.

(177)
$C = (\alpha_1,...,\alpha_n)$ is a *chain* if and only if
a. α_i locally A-binds α_{i+1};
b. for $i > 1$, (i) α_i is a nonpronominal empty category
           or (ii) α_i is A-free;
c. C is maximal (i.e., is not a proper subsequence of a chain meeting (a) and (b)).

Case (177bi) of this simplified definition of chain singles out the pronominal empty category and virtually amounts to saying that PRO must be head of the chain. Consider, for instance, the following structure:

(178)
John$_i$ wants [$_\bar{S}$[$_S$ PRO$_i$ to leave]]

Here, PRO is coindexed with *John*, which is in an A-position; it is not A-free. By clause (177bii), *John* and PRO must be taken to be in distinct chains, each of which is assigned a distinct θ-role. Suppose they were in the same chain: PRO would receive a θ-role from the embedded predicate, and *John* would receive one from the matrix VP. The derivation would be ruled out by the θ-Criterion—redefined as a well-formedness condition on chains—since two θ-roles would be assigned to the same chain.

We will take this redundancy between the Visibility Convention and the definition of chain to indicate a deficiency—at least in the definition of these notions—that we will seek to eliminate. The assumption according to which $\bar{S}$ breaks an A-chain accomplishes this task. Consider again (178) and its two chains, the first containing *John* and the second PRO. Given that PRO must be ungoverned, it cannot be in a context of $\bar{S}$-Deletion. Thus, by assuming that $\bar{S}$ breaks a chain, we obtain the correct result in (178): PRO and *John* will be in different chains.

We can now eliminate the redundancy between the Visibility Convention and the definition of chain:

(179)

$C = (\alpha_1,...,\alpha_n)$ is a *chain* if and only if

a. α_i locally A-binds α_{i+1};

b. for $i > 1$, α_i is A-free if not empty;

c. $\bar{S}$ does not intervene between α_i and α_{i+1};

d. C is maximal (i.e., is not proper subsequence of a chain meeting (a)–(c)).

2.10.3 $\bar{S}$-Deletion and the *i*-within-*i* Condition

The assumption that $\bar{S}$ breaks a chain allows us to account for cases of NP-traces covered by the ECP, and it may rule out some cases of improper movement and eliminate some redundancies between interacting principles such as the Visibility Convention and the notion of chain. We may now ask, Is it possible to further motivate the existence of such an assumption by relating it to more general principles at work in the grammar?

This question may be answered if we assume the following characterization of $\bar{S}$-Deletion. Adopting the analysis of impersonal constructions given in LGB, M.-L. Zubizarreta (1982) assumes that the impersonal subject position and the clause are coindexed—more precisely, cosuperscripted. (The exact nature of this coindexing mechanism is not relevant to our discussion.) Consider the following examples:

(180)

a. it^i seems [$_{\bar{S}^i}$ that John is sick]

b. it^i is probable [$_{\bar{S}^i}$ that John is sick]

When the embedded subject moves into the matrix subject position, the following structures will result:

(181)

a. John$_j^i$ seems [$_{\bar{S}^i}$ t_j^i to be sick]

b. *John$_j^i$ is probable [$_{\bar{S}^i}$ t_j^i to be sick]

Representations (181a–b) clearly violate the *i*-within-*i* Condition. However, raising verbs like *seem* trigger $\bar{S}$-Deletion, after which (181a) will have the following representation:

(182)

John$_j^i$ seems [$_S$ e_j^i to be sick]

Thus, deleting $\bar{S}$ avoids a violation of the *i*-within-*i* Condition. For Zubizarreta's argument to succeed, it is necessary to assume that the process of $\bar{S}$-Transparency deletes $\bar{S}$ rather than rewriting $\bar{S}$ as S, as was assumed in section 2.9. Another possibility would be to maintain that $\bar{S}$-Transparency rewrites $\bar{S}$ as S and erases the indices of $\bar{S}$. In brief, Zubizarreta assumes that the *raison d'être* of $\bar{S}$-Deletion in the case of raising constructions is to avoid a violation of the *i*-within-*i* Condition.

However, although the *i*-within-*i* Condition may motivate the existence of $\bar{S}$-Deletion in raising constructions, it cannot motivate all cases of $\bar{S}$-Deletion. There are constructions where $\bar{S}$ is deleted and where the *i*-within-*i* Condition seems irrelevant. After *believe*-type verbs, for instance, $\bar{S}$-Deletion applies:

(183)
a. John believes [$_{\bar{S}}$ that Bill is a fool]
b. John believes [$_S$ Bill to be a fool]

Here, since $\bar{S}$ is deleted, *believe* governs and assigns Case to the subject of the embedded clause.

Thus, there are instances where the *i*-within-*i* Condition is irrelevant to $\bar{S}$-Deletion, though this does not mean that $\bar{S}$-Deletion is irrelevant with respect to the *i*-within-*i* Condition. That is, Zubizarreta's analysis of constructions (181a–b) and (182) (that $\bar{S}$-Deletion helps to prevent an *i*-within-*i* Condition violation) can be maintained, but not the view that the sole function of $\bar{S}$-Deletion is to avoid a violation of that condition.

2.11 Summary

In this chapter we first considered some empirical and conceptual problems in the GB framework. Empirically, the extraction of *wh*-elements from inside an NP in Italian and French indicates that—contrary to GB theory assumptions—the SSC does apply to variables. The conceptual problems involve redundancies between the binding theory and the ECP: essentially, both require an antecedent for the NP-trace. To overcome these problems, we rearranged certain elements of the GB framework. In GB theory, variables must be A-free by the binding principles and $\bar{A}$-bound (or more precisely properly governed) by the ECP. These different requirements can be brought together by generalizing the binding theory from a theory of A-binding to a theory of X-binding (where X = A or $\bar{A}$), as follows: for empty elements, the definition of anaphors now includes variables; as anaphors, variables will be subject to principle (A) of the binding theory (which requires anaphors to be X-bound in their governing category). As placeholders for names, they will also be subject to binding principle (C) (which requires names to be A-free). To satisfy both principles, X-bound must be taken to mean $\bar{\text{A}}$-bound; variables must be $\bar{\text{A}}$-bound in their governing category. This modification accounts for the extraction of *wh*-elements from inside an NP in Italian, French, and Hebrew and thus solves the aforementioned empirical problems. As for the conceptual problems, the effect of this modification is to increase them. In the GB framework, since the binding theory is a theory of A-binding, the redundancy between the binding principles and the ECP is restricted to NP-traces. When the binding theory is generalized to a theory of X-binding, the redundancy is extended to variables: both the binding theory and the ECP require variables to have an antecedent. Clearly, the solution is to eliminate the ECP; and this we have accomplished.

For variables, the elimination is straightforward: the cases covered by the ECP are also covered by the generalized binding principles. For NP-traces, the binding principles are irrelevant: in the derivations filtered out by the ECP, the trace is not governed and hence lacks a governing category. Binding principle (A), which requires an NP-trace to be bound in its governing category, is thus inoperative. The θ-Criterion, however, accounts for the instances of NP-traces covered by the ECP. We modified the definition of chain and restricted its domain to $\bar{\text{S}}$. Consequently, in the derivations covered by the ECP, the trace and its antecedent will be in different chains. Since by the Projection Principle and the θ-Criterion the antecedent of a trace is in a non-θ-position, it will not receive a θ-role and the derivation will be filtered out by the θ-Criterion. In this account the ECP is a spurious generalization; the RES(NIC) cases accounted for by this principle do not constitute a unified phenomenon. Non–properly governed variables are excluded by the binding principles and non–properly governed traces by the θ-Criterion.

Chapter 3
Anaphors, Pronouns, and Nonovert Categories

The elimination of the ECP was partially made possible by generalizing the binding theory to a theory of A-binding and $\overline{\text{A}}$-binding. Since the ECP is taken to apply at LF (Kayne 1981b), the generalized binding theory will have to apply at LF. In this chapter we will consider evidence from various LF processes that supports this conclusion, as well as evidence showing that the binding principles also apply at S-structure. In short, it will appear that the generalized binding principles apply at the output of each component where anaphoric relations are determined—namely, both at S-structure and at LF.

The analysis of the LF processes relevant to the application of the binding theory will bear on the characterization of such fundamental elements as anaphors, pronominals, and empty categories. I will suggest characterizing anaphors in terms of an incomplete matrix. I will also argue that pronominals are generated as a set of features and that they are phonetically realized as pronouns in PF when they are Case-governed; otherwise, they are interpreted as PRO. Pronominal elements thus will be distinguished with respect to Case-government: if a pronominal is Case-governed, it will be interpreted as a pronoun (*he, she,* etc.); otherwise, it will be interpreted as PRO.

The theoretical implication of this proposal concerning pronominals will be a reinterpretation of the notion "empty category" defined in GB theory. I will suggest that *there is no type distinction between pronouns and the so-called empty (nonovert) categories (NP-trace,* wh-*trace, PRO).* Pronouns are just a different occurrence of the "empty category" identified as such in terms of properties of the structure they appear in. I will propose a typology of the empty category that includes nonovert $\overline{\text{A}}$-anaphors and will test its empirical adequacy with respect to one that does not.

Turning to the interpretation of empty elements, I will characterize the conditions under which a nonovert element functions as an argument bearing a θ-role. In particular, I will distinguish two kinds of nonovert $\overline{A}$-anaphors: nonovert $\overline{A}$-anaphors that bear an independent θ-role (e.g., *wh*-traces) and nonovert $\overline{A}$-anaphors that do not bear an independent θ-role (e.g., the gaps coindexed with clitics). Only the former will be treated as arguments with respect to the θ-theory and the binding theory.

3.1 The Logical Nature of the Binding Theory

3.1.1 Lowering of *There*
It has been observed (Dresher and Hornstein 1979, attributed to Postal) that *there* can only be moved once. Thus, (1a), where *there* has been moved once, contrasts with (1b), where it has been moved twice:

(1)
a.   there seems to be someone in the room
b.   ?*there seems to be likely to be someone in the room

(2)
a. $[_{S_1}$ there$_1$ seems $[_{S_2}$ e_2 to be someone in the room]]
b. $[_{S_1}$ there$_1$ seems $[_{S_2}$ e_2 to be likely $[_{S_3}$ e_3 to be someone in the room]]]
     (where e is the trace left by the extraction rule)

As indicated in section 2.10, it is assumed that *there* and the postverbal NP form a chain. To account for the contrast between (1a) and (1b), we will make the following assumptions as well:

(3)
a.   In LF, *there* is lowered to the minimal clause (S) containing the element with which it forms a chain.
b.   In raising constructions, there is a process inserting a dummy nonreferential PRO in nominative contexts (or more generally in Case-governed contexts. We will return to the exact formulation later on).

Nonreferential PRO is the phonetically unrealized counterpart of nonreferential *it: it seems that Peter likes John*. Given assumptions (3a–b), the contrast between (1a) and (1b) will be accounted for by the binding principles.

Consider the derivation of (1b). First *there* is lowered:

(4)

$[_{\bar{S}_1}[_{S_1} e_1 \text{ seems } [_{S_2} e_2 \text{ to be likely } [_{S_3} \text{ there}_3 \text{ to be someone in the room}]]]]$

Then the dummy element is inserted:

(5)

$[_{\bar{S}_1}[_{S_1} \text{ PRO}_1 \text{ seems } [_{S_2} e_2 \text{ to be likely } [_{S_3} \text{ there}_3 \text{ to be someone in the room}]]]]$

It is possible to think of Lowering as undoing the effect of Move α. If this is the case, then in (4), which is generated from (2b) by Lowering, *there* and the two empty elements will no longer be coindexed as they were in (2b). In other words, e_1 in (4), or for that matter the PRO that is inserted in the position of e_1 in (5), will not count as the antecedent of the trace e_2. Derivation (4)–(5) will be ruled out by the binding principles: the minimal clause containing a governor (*seems*) and an accessible SUBJECT (the matrix AGR) for e_2 is the matrix clause. In this governing category e_2 is A-free, violating binding principle (A).

For this analysis to be valid, it is necessary that PRO and the empty element e_2 in (5) not be reindexed by free indexing. I will argue in section 3.7 that A-indexing (indexing between elements in A-position) does not apply at LF. This automatically will prevent PRO and e_2 from being reindexed at LF since these elements are in A-position. Note that we need not assume that Lowering applies in a successive fashion. Let us assume instead that *there* in (4) is lowered to the subject position of S_3 in one move. Since Lowering undoes the effect of Move α, the subject position of the matrix clause will lose its index. In that case (5) will have the following representation after PRO-Insertion:

(6)

$[_{\bar{S}}[_{S_1} \text{ PRO seems } [_{S_2} e_i \text{ to be likely } [\text{there}_i \text{ to be someone in the room}]]]]$

Here, even though the intermediate trace has an index, it has no c-commanding antecedent, and the binding principles are still violated. Finally, there are speakers who accept (1b). Unlike *there*, *it* can be raised twice:

(7)

it$_i$ is expected e_i to appear e_i to be likely that John will come

It may be that for these speakers *there* is treated like *it* and need not be lowered; see section 5.4 for relevant considerations.

Now consider (1a). For this representation, the binding theory is irrelevant. After the lowering of *there* and the insertion of the dummy element, (1a) will have the following representation:

(8)
[$_{\bar{S}_1}$ PRO seems [$_{S_2}$ there$_2$ to be someone in the room]]

No binding violation occurs in (8).

3.1.2 Quantifier-Lowering
The analysis suggested to account for the ungrammaticality of doubly raised *there* may be extended to account for some cases of Quantifier-Lowering. Consider the following sentence discussed in May 1977:

(9)
some politician is likely to address John's constituency

May argues that this sentence is ambiguous: the quantifier may be understood as having either wider or narrower scope than the matrix predicate. It may be taken as asserting either (a) that there is a politician (e.g., Rockefeller) who is likely to address John's constituency, or (b) that it is likely that there is some politician (or other) who will address John's constituency:

(10)
a. there is a politician S, such that it is likely that S addresses John's constituency
b. it is likely that there is a politician S, such that S addresses John's constituency

May explains these judgments in terms of his rule of Quantifier-Movement, which, he suggests, can "lower" the quantifier. It is thus possible to derive two logical forms from the S-structure of (9): one by adjoining the quantified NP *some politician* to the matrix S, the other by lowering and adjoining it to the embedded S:

(11)
a. [$_{S_1}$ some politician [$_S$ e_1 is likely [$_{S_2}$ e_2 to address John's constituency]]]
b. [$_{S_1}$ e_1 is likely [$_{S_2}$ some politician [$_S$ e_2 to address John's constituency]]]

Now consider the following sentence, where the quantified NP has been raised twice in Syntax:

(12)
some politician seems to be likely to address John's constituency

As has been noticed, (12) is not ambiguous: it may be taken as asserting
(a) that there is a politician (e.g., Rockefeller) who seems to be likely to
address John's constituency, but not (b) that it seems to be likely that
there is some politician (or other) who will address John's constituency
(the judgments are those of N. Chomsky, J. Higginbotham, and J.-R.
Vergnaud (for the corresponding French examples)):

(13)
a. there is a politician S such that it seems to be likely that S ad-
    dresses John's constituency
b. *it seems to be likely that there is a politician S such that S ad-
    dresses John's constituency

Clearly, the paradigm considered in (9) through (13) is parallel to the
one considered in the preceding section. The analysis suggested concerning the lowering of *there* may be extended to quantifiers (we will
return later to the formulation of these statements):

(14)
a. In LF, a quantifier may be lowered.
b. In raising constructions, there is a process inserting a dummy
    nonreferential PRO in nominative contexts.

Given assumptions (14a–b), the nonambiguity of (12) may be accounted
for by the binding theory. Consider the representation of the two possible readings of (12): (15a–b) correspond to (13a–b), respectively. We
will disregard the intermediate reading where *some politician* is lowered and attached to the intermediate S; it is irrelevant for our purposes.
(For helpful discussions, I wish to thank M. Rooth, who examines the
parallelism between doubly raised *there* and doubly raised quantifiers
in an unpublished study carried out in a Montague framework.)

(15)
a. $[_{S_1}$ some politician $[_{S_1}$ e_1 seems $[_{S_2}$ e_2 to be likely $[_{S_3}$ e_3 to address
    John's constituency]]]]
b. $[_{S_1}$ PRO_1 seems $[_{S_2}$ e_2 to be likely $[_{S_3}$ some politician $[_{S_3}$ e_3 to address
    John's constituency]]]]

In (15b) the quantifier has been lowered and adjoined to the embedded
S_3 by the two processes of Quantifier-Lowering (see (14a)) and Quantifier-Raising (May 1977), and a dummy PRO has been inserted in the

subject position of S_1 (see (14b)). In (15a–b) the minimal clause containing a governor (*seems*) and an accessible SUBJECT (AGR of the matrix clause) for e_2 is the matrix clause. In this category, e_2 is A-free in (15b) but A-bound by e_1 in (15a). Consequently, (15b)—but not (15a)—will be ruled out by principle (A) of the binding theory.

In (11a–b), however, no violation of the binding principles occurs. In (11b) the dummy PRO will be inserted in e_1 according to (14b). In (11a) e_2 will be bound by e_1 and e_1 will be bound by *some politician;* and in (11b) e_2 will be bound by *some politician*. In short, the nonambiguity of (12) versus the ambiguity of (9) is accounted for by the binding theory: whereas the structures corresponding to the two readings of (9) do not violate any grammatical principles, the narrow-scope reading of (12) (namely, (15b)) violates the binding theory.

Thus, the proposed analyses of *there* and of the lowered quantifier provide further evidence for the LF character of the binding theory since at S-structure (i.e., before Lowering) no binding theory violation occurs: the binding principles must apply at the output of the LF rule of Lowering.

3.1.3 Remarks on Lowering

The analysis of doubly raised *there* and of Quantifier-Lowering clearly raises many questions. It is legitimate to ask when Lowering is possible, when the process of dummy insertion operates, what the exact nature of the inserted element is, and so on. To answer these and other questions of related interest will be the main concern of this section.

Let us start by considering the various assumptions made in the previous two sections:

(16)
a. In LF, *there* is lowered to the minimal clause (S) containing the element with which it forms a chain.
b. In raising constructions, there is a process inserting a dummy nonreferential PRO in nominative contexts.

(17)
a. In LF, a quantifier may be lowered.
b. In raising constructions, there is a process inserting a dummy nonreferential PRO in nominative contexts.

The context in which the dummy element is inserted need not be restricted to nominative contexts. It can be generalized to Case-governed contexts, that is, to contexts where a governor assigns Case: after *believe*-type verbs, for instance, which govern and assign Case to the embedded subject, the same facts discussed in the previous two sections hold, as illustrated in (18a–b). Later the process of PRO-Insertion will be dispensed with (section 3.4).

(18)
a.   I believe there to seem to be someone in the room
b.   ?*I believe there to seem to be likely to be someone in the room

(19)
I believe some politician to be likely to address John's constituency

(20)
I believe some politician to seem to be likely to address John's constituency

Lowering itself does not seem to be possible in all constructions. As indicated in May 1977, it does not apply in *want*-type constructions. In contrast with (21), (22a) is unambiguously interpreted as (22b); the reading where the quantifier has narrower scope than the matrix predicate is not available:

(21)
some politician is likely to address John's constituency

(22)
a. some politician wants to address John's constituency
b. there is a politician S, such that S wants that S addresses John's constituency

Raising constructions such as (21) differ from *want*-type constructions such as (22a) in that $\bar{\text{S}}$-Deletion applies in the former, permitting the embedded subject to be raised:

(23)
some politician$_i$ is likely [$_S$ e_i to address John's constituency]

(24)
some politician$_i$ wants [$_{\bar{S}}$[$_S$ PRO$_i$ to address John's constituency]]

As indicated in LGB (p. 177), the process of Quantifier-Lowering thus distinguishes between PRO and trace and provides further evidence for the distinction between these two empty elements. In terms of the definition of chain suggested in chapter 2, the quantifier and its trace *e* in (23) are in the same chain, whereas the quantifier and PRO in (24) are in different chains, being separated by $\bar{\text{S}}$. It is therefore natural to suggest that chains constitute the domain in which Lowering may apply. This suggestion will provide the adequate distinction between (23) and (24), while allowing *there* to be lowered in sentences such as (18a).

Can this result—that chains constitute the domain in which Lowering applies—be derived from existing grammatical principles? Suppose that Lowering were to apply in a construction like (24). After Lowering and PRO-Insertion, (24) would have the following LF representation:

(25)
PRO wants [$_{\bar{\text{s}}}$ some politician to address John's constituency]

Note first that the pronominal element in (25) must be referential, since it is inserted in a θ-position; otherwise, the θ-Criterion would be violated. Second, *some politician,* or the variable it binds, is assigned a different θ-role at LF from the one assigned at S-structure: at S-structure it receives its θ-role from the matrix predicate, and at LF it receives its θ-role from the embedded predicate. The Projection Principle, which is essentially a conservation principle and requires the *same* θ-role to be assigned to an element at D-structure, S-structure, and LF, would be violated (see LGB (chapter 2) and Chomsky 1982 for further details concerning this principle). Thus, if Lowering were to apply in control constructions such as (24), the Projection Principle would be violated.

Now consider raising constructions such as (21). After Lowering and PRO-Insertion, (21) will have the following LF representation:

(26)
PRO is likely some politician to address John's constituency

In (26) the pronominal element must not be referential, since it is not in a θ-position; otherwise, the θ-Criterion would be violated. It thus appears that the referential status of PRO in (25) and (26) need not be stipulated; it follows from the θ-Criterion. Moreover, in (26) (contrary to (25)) no Projection Principle violation occurs, since *some politician,* or the variable it binds, will be assigned the same θ-role at S-structure and at LF: at both levels, it will receive its θ-role from the embedded predicate. In short, the fact that chains constitute the domain in which Lowering applies need not be stipulated; it follows from the Projection Principle.

3.2 The PRO/Pronoun Distinction

Another question raised by the analysis of the previous sections concerns the dummy element that was assimilated to a nonreferential PRO—the phonetically unrealized counterpart of the nonreferential *it*. The identification of this dummy element presents a major problem. From the binding theory, it follows that PRO must be ungoverned: if the dummy element were PRO, the output of the insertion rule would have to be filtered out by the binding theory, since this PRO is inserted in a Case-governed context. An ad hoc solution would be to consider that this expletive element is not a PRO (hence not subject to the binding theory) or, worse, that (unlike the referential PRO) an expletive PRO must not be ungoverned. For various empirical and theoretical reasons mentioned in LGB (chapter 6), this proposal cannot be maintained. Briefly, it appears to be desirable to keep as much as possible the parallelism between phonetically realized and phonetically unrealized nominal elements: phonetically unrealized elements differ from phonetically realized elements in that they lack a phonetic matrix. Phonetically realized elements may be referential or not; similarly, phonetically unrealized elements will be referential or not. Nominal elements may thus be classified with respect to the features [±referential], [±overt]. (In LGB (p. 325) it is argued that this classification is to be refined to include quasi-arguments. This, however, is not relevant for our purposes.)

(27)
a. [+referential, −overt]: PRO
   (as in *John wants* [$_{\bar{s}}$ *PRO to win*])
b. [+referential, +overt]: lexical names and pronouns
   (*John; he, she*)
c. [−referential, +overt]: expletive elements
   (*it* in *it seems that John is sick; there;* etc.)
d. [−referential, −overt]: phonetically unrealized expletive elements
   (dummy PROs)

Furthermore, in Aoun 1982 it is argued that expletive PROs cannot appear in governed contexts.

   The above considerations prevent us from considering that the dummy element inserted is not a PRO or that it need not be ungoverned. Let us therefore consider a more principled approach to the problem raised by the occurrence of the nonreferential PRO in Case-governed contexts.

Recall that in the GB framework lexical insertion rules and base rules generate D-structures, which are mapped into S-structures by Move α. S-structures are in turn mapped into the two interpretive components PF (= Phonetic Form) and LF (= Logical Form), yielding Surface-structures and LF-structures, respectively.

PRO is a set of features (αperson, βnumber, γgender, etc.). It differs from other pronouns in that it lacks a phonetic matrix. I will assume that pronouns are always generated as a set of features (αperson, βnumber, γgender) and that they are phonetically realized in PF when they are Case-governed. Thus, pronominal elements are distinguished with respect to Case-government: if a pronominal is Case-governed, it is interpreted as a pronoun; otherwise, it is interpreted as PRO. To illustrate, the pronominal subject of the sentence *he likes Mary* would in fact be generated as a set of features (masculine, singular, 3rd person, etc.) in subject position. Since this feature matrix receives nominative Case, it will be phonetically realized as a pronoun. A similar proposal for the phonetic realization of pronouns was first suggested in Jaeggli 1982:

(28)
Pronounce PRO if it has Case and is c-governed (= categorial government).

Both proposals are to be embodied in the general Visibility Convention suggested in Aoun 1979 according to which Case is the relevant feature in PF: in order for an element to be visible in PF, it must be Case-marked.

With respect to the principles at work in the grammar, the distinction is thus between Case-governed and non-Case-governed pronominals: a Case-governed pronominal is subject to binding principle (B), whereas a non-Case-governed pronominal is subject to binding principles (A) and (B); a Case-governed pronominal must be free in its governing category, whereas a non-Case-governed pronominal or PRO must be ungoverned. For instance, consider gerunds and NPs:

(29)
a. [$_{NP}$ NP* VP]
b. [$_{NP}$ NP* $\bar{N}$]

Under the definition of government adopted in chapter 2, the head of VP in (29a) does not govern NP* since it is dominated by a maximal projection (namely, VP) that does not dominate NP*. But the head of $\overline{N}$ in (29b) does govern NP*, since NP is the first maximal projection dominating NP* and the head of $\overline{N}$. Let us consider that Case assignment is optional and that the set of features [αperson, βnumber, γgender] may be freely inserted in NP* position. In (29a), if we choose to assign Case to NP*, this set of features will be Case-marked (hence, phonetically realized); otherwise, it will not have a phonetic matrix:

(30)
a. I like [$_{NP}$ PRO reading books]
b. I like [$_{NP}$ his reading books]

In (29b), if we choose to assign Case to NP*, the set of features will be Case-marked (hence, phonetically realized in PF); if we choose not to assign Case, the non-Case-marked PRO will have to be ungoverned, thus precluding its occurrence as the subject of the NP:

(31)
a. I like [$_{NP}$ his book]
b. I like [$_{NP}$ PRO book]

This approach solves the problem raised by the insertion of a dummy PRO in Case-governed contexts in raising constructions. Recall that this dummy PRO is inserted in the subject position of the matrix clause that is Case-governed by AGR, as in (32):

(32)
PRO AGR V [NP V ...]

Being Case-governed by AGR, this element will be subject not to principles (A) and (B) of the binding theory, but only to principle (B): it does not need to be ungoverned. The only peculiarity of this element is that it is inserted in LF, after the application of the Lowering rules. Since it is inserted in LF, the PF rules that phonetically spell out Case-marked pronominals will not apply to it.

3.3 The Nature of Anaphors

We may wonder why non-Case-governed pronominals are treated as anaphors. This amounts to asking, What is an anaphor? In the GB framework anaphors such as reciprocals and reflexives are considered to lack inherent reference. We may assume, as in LGB section 3.2.3, that these elements are potentially referential and that they pick up their actual reference by virtue of being coindexed with an antecedent. This is why they need an antecedent. This assumption is not redundant with the binding theory. These reflexives and reciprocals must be bound by an antecedent in order to have their actual reference. What the binding theory determines is the domain in which they must be bound: the governing category.

However, it cannot be maintained that the notion of reference is relevant to all anaphors. There are anaphors such as NP-trace that do not pick any reference from an antecedent. The most extreme case is that of an NP-trace whose antecedent is not even referential:

(33)
a. it$_i$ seems t_i to be certain that John left
b. there$_i$ seems t_i to be someone in the room

In (33a–b) the antecedent of the trace is not referential. It is therefore meaningless to say that this trace picks its actual reference from its antecedent. Moreover, PRO is an anaphor, and there are constructions where this pronominal anaphor has no antecedent:

(34)
[PRO to leave] is difficult

It thus appears that the notion of anaphora must be general enough to allow nonreferential elements to be treated as anaphors. Obviously, we do not want all nonreferential elements to be treated as anaphors; otherwise, for instance, *it* in (33a) will be characterized as an anaphor.

With this in mind, let us return to the distinction between pronouns and PROs suggested in the previous section. The only difference between pronouns and PROs is that the former but not the latter are Case-governed:

(35)
a. Pronouns: [+pronominal, +Case-governed]
b. PROs: [+pronominal, −Case-governed]

Thus, by virtue of not being Case-governed, a pronominal element is treated as an anaphor:

(36)
a. Pronouns are Case-governed and are therefore not anaphoric.
b. PROs are not Case-governed and are therefore anaphoric.

Given that we assume that PROs differ minimally from pronouns in that they are not Case-governed and that some PROs are not even referential, it is possible to assume that every element with an incomplete matrix is treated as an anaphor: tautologically, a matrix is incomplete if it is not fully specified for all the relevant features such as referentiality, Case-government, etc. Reflexives and reciprocals are anaphors since they lack inherent reference: their referentiality is not fully specified. PROs and NP-traces are anaphors since they are not Case-governed. A nonreferential *it* such as the one in (33a) is not an anaphor, since it is Case-governed and [−referential]: the relevant features are fully specified.

As for *wh*-traces, we have distinguished PROs from pronouns by the feature [±Case-governed]. In the GB framework, PROs, *wh*-traces, and NP-traces are considered to be three occurrences of the same type: they all have the features [αperson, βnumber, γgender], but they differ with respect to their antecedent:

(37)
Functional Characterization of Empty Categories
a. Gaps with antecedents that lack an independent θ-role
    (i) and are locally A-bound (= NP-traces)
    (ii) and are locally $\bar{\text{A}}$-bound (= variables)
b. Gaps with antecedents that have an independent θ-role (= PROs)
c. Gaps with no antecedents (= PROs)

Furthermore, it is assumed that *wh*-traces are Case-governed, whereas PROs and NP-traces are not. In short, PROs and *wh*-traces differ with respect to Case-government. Given our earlier discussion of the phonetic realization of pronouns, we would expect *wh*-traces to be phonetically realized, since they are Case-governed. Although the process is restricted, *wh*-traces may in fact be phonetically realized in various languages such as Arabic, Hebrew, and Vata (Aoun 1979, Borer 1979, Koopman 1980). Case-government is a necessary but not a sufficient condition for an element to be phonetically realized. Thus, for an element to be phonetically realized in English, it must be Case-governed and must not be marked [+wh] (that is, it must not be coindexed with a *wh*-element); only non-Case-marked pronominals are phonetically realized in this language. However, with respect to the Visibility Convention of Aoun 1979, Case seems to be a sufficient condition for an element to be visible in PF: *wh*-traces, for instance, which are Case-governed, play a role in PF mechanisms such as contraction. (See

Lightfoot 1977, Jaeggli 1980, and the references mentioned there for an attempt to generalize the visibility of empty elements from *wh*-traces to all categories; also see Pesetsky 1982b.)

As for NP-traces, there seems to be no clear case where these elements are spelled out as pronouns. Given that they are not Case-marked, this is not surprising. L. Burzio (1981) suggests that such a situation seems to occur; however, it seems that the constructions he discusses are instances of apposition rather than instances of the realization of NP-trace.

Returning to *wh*-traces, the discussion of anaphors raises an interesting question with respect to the status of these elements: why are they treated as ($\bar{\text{A}}$-)anaphors? There are at least two possibilities: that variables are anaphors because they lack inherent reference, or that variables are anaphors when they are not phonetically realized. The two possibilities make different predictions, and it appears that the second is to be preferred. As indicated in Koopman 1980, Aoun 1979, and Aoun 1981a, variables left by the extraction of *wh*-elements are subject to the ECP in languages such as Vata, Modern Hebrew, and Arabic. If these variables are phonetically spelled out, however, they escape the effect of the ECP. Thus, consider the following sentences of Arabic:

(38)
a. *man_i taḏunnu   ʔanna x_i ðahaba
   who_i do you think that e_i left
b. man_i taḏunnu   ʔannahu$_i$ ðahaba
   who_i do you think that he$_i$ left
   'who do you think left'

(38a) illustrates a *[*that-t*] effect; the variable is not properly governed and is thus ruled out by the ECP. In (38b), however, where the variable is phonetically spelled out, no ECP violation occurs. In the framework of chapter 1, this amounts to saying that only the variable in (38a) is treated as an anaphor. This variable will therefore be subject to binding principles (A) and (C) and as such will display a *[*that-t*] effect. However, the variable in (38b) will not be treated as an anaphor and as such will not display a *[*that-t*] effect. It is to be mentioned that unlike normal resumptive pronouns, the spelled-out variables do obey the usual constraints on movement such as the Complex NP Constraint (Aoun 1981).

With this in mind, let us return to the two possibilities concerning variables. The first, that variables are anaphors because they lack inherent reference, will treat both variables in (38a) and (38b) as anaphors and thus will not be able to account for the contrast between the two sentences. The second possibility, however, encounters no such problem. It will correctly treat the variable in (38a) as an anaphor because it is not phonetically realized; the one in (38b), however, will not be treated as an anaphor.

In brief, Case-government seems to be a necessary and sufficient condition for pronouns to be phonetically realized. As such, they are not anaphors. On the other hand, in some languages Case-government does not seem to be a sufficient condition for *wh*-traces to be phonetically realized. When they are not or cannot be phonetically realized, these elements are treated as anaphors. In other words, an element is an anaphor (= has an incomplete matrix) if it lacks an inherent reference (reflexives, reciprocals) or if it does not satisfy the necessary conditions for phonetic realization (NP-traces, *wh*-traces, PROs).

3.4 Insertion Rules

The Lowering analysis presented in section 3.1 involves a process of nonovert pronominal insertion that deserves further comment. The empty element left in the position from which Lowering applies (*e* in (39b)) will be left free, thus violating the binding theory, which requires empty elements such as NP-traces to be locally bound:

(39)
a. NP_i AGR V $[_S e_i$ V ...] $\xrightarrow{\text{by Lowering}}$
b. *e* AGR V $[_S$ NP V ...]

Derivations such as (39a–b), however, are saved by a process inserting a nonreferential pronominal in Case-governed contexts. This inserted element "absorbs" the free empty element and (like all Case-marked pronominals) need not be ungoverned:

(39)
c. PRO AGR $[_S$ NP V ...]

Since the insertion process is limited to Case-governed contexts, it follows that an element that has been moved twice in Syntax will not be lowered in LF to its base-generated position (e_2 in (40a)):

(40)

a.   NP AGR V $[_{S_1} e_1$ V $[_{S_2} e_2$ V ...$]]$ $\xrightarrow[\text{and PRO-Insertion}]{\text{by Lowering}}$

b.   *PRO AGR V $[_{S_1} e_1$ V $[_{S_2}$ NP$_2$ V ...$]]$

Were it lowered in this way, as in (40b), the intermediate empty element e_1 would be left free, and the structure would be ruled out.

Why is the process of pronominal insertion restricted to Case-governed contexts? Is it possible to dispense with any restriction concerning insertion processes? Obviously, the most radical way to dispense with any restriction concerning insertion processes is to eliminate the need for the insertion rule. Recall the functional characterization of empty elements given in section 3.3: empty elements are considered to be three occurrences of the same type, but they differ with respect to their antecedent (if any).

With this in mind, consider once again derivation (39a–c). As indicated earlier, the NP may be lowered to the position of its trace; subsequently, the empty element left in the position from which Lowering applies will be absorbed by the inserted nonreferential pronominal. The insertion rule can now be dispensed with: in (39b) the empty element is free. According to the functional definition of empty categories, it will be interpreted as a pronominal. This pronominal is in a Case-governed context; it is subject only to binding principle (B).

As for doubly raised elements, we have seen that the NP may be lowered to the position of the intermediate trace e_1 but not to that of e_2 (see (40a–b)):

(41)

$*e$ AGR V $[_{S_1} e_1$ V $[_{S_2}$ NP V ...$]]$

We have accounted for the ungrammaticality of (41) by restricting the insertion rule to Case-governed contexts: e will be absorbed by the inserted pronominal, but not e_1. Furthermore, since Lowering undoes the effect of Move α, the inserted pronominal will not be coindexed with e_1; it cannot function as the binder of e_1. The insertion rule having been eliminated, this solution is no longer available. However, the functional characterization of empty categories provides a natural way to account for (41). In this construction both empty elements are free; they will both be interpreted as pronominals. The pronominal in the subject position of the matrix clause is in a Case-governed context and is subject only to principle (B) of the binding theory. However, the pronominal in the intermediate clause S_1 is not in a Case-governed

context. Like all non-Case-governed pronominals, it is treated as an
anaphor. As a pronominal it is subject to principle (B) of the binding
theory, and as an anaphor it is subject to principle (A). The only way to
satisfy both principles is for this element to be ungoverned. This is not
the case in (41): e_1 is governed by the matrix V. Therefore, the representation will be ruled out.

3.5 A Typology of Empty Categories

3.5.1 PRO: Non-Case-governed or Non-Case-marked?

I have been using the term *Case-government* and have suggested that a
pronominal is anaphoric (PRO) if it is not Case-governed. However, I
have not said that a pronominal is anaphoric (PRO) if it is not Case-
marked. The reason for using Case-government is that strictly speaking, an anaphoric pronominal (PRO) may be Case-marked. Consider
again representation (41),

(41)
$*e$ AGR V [$_{S_1}$ e_1 V [$_{S_2}$ NP V ...]]

where the intermediate empty element e_1—unlike the matrix empty
element e—is not in a Case-governed context. Both empty elements
are free; hence, they will be identified as pronominals. Being in a Case-
governed context, e will be characterized as a pronoun; it is subject
only to binding principle (B). e_1 will be characterized as an anaphoric
pronominal, PRO; it is subject to binding principles (A) and (B) and
must be ungoverned to satisfy both principles. Now, instead of assuming that a non-Case-governed pronominal is an anaphor, is it possible to
assume that a non-Case-marked pronominal is an anaphor? In other
words, is it possible to suggest that PRO is a non-Case-marked rather
than a non-Case-governed pronominal? The answer is no. In GB theory
the Case-feature is assigned to a chain as a whole if a member of the
chain is in a Case-governed position (see section 2.10 and LGB, chapter
6). In (41), therefore, assuming that after Lowering the empty elements
e and e_1—and irrelevantly the lowered NP—still form a chain, they
will be Case-marked by virtue of being in a chain containing an element
in a Case-governed position: the matrix empty element. If we were to
assume that PRO is non-Case-marked instead of non-Case-governed,
both empty elements e and e_1 would be identified as pronouns. We
would have no way to account for the ungrammaticality of (41). Hence
the assumption that PRO is non-Case-governed instead of non-Case-

marked. Other instances of Case-marked PROs in Warlpiri and Icelandic are discussed in Simpson 1982.

Similar considerations hold for NP-traces. NP-trace is an anaphor because it cannot be phonetically realized. It cannot be phonetically realized because it is not Case-governed:

(42)
John$_i$ seems t_i to have left

Once again, we cannot suggest that it cannot be phonetically realized because it is not Case-marked. By virtue of being in a chain containing a Case-governed position, it will be Case-marked. In (42) the NP-trace is Case-marked because the other member of the chain, *John,* is in a Case-governed position.

Relevant in this respect is the Case Visibility Principle of Levin 1983. According to this principle, Case is visible only under government. Levin's principle reveals why a Case-governed pronominal, and not a Case-marked pronominal, is interpreted as a pronoun: the Case-feature of a Case-marked ungoverned pronominal will not be visible according to the Case Visibility Principle. (Note that this principle is relevant at LF, since pronominals generated by the LF process of Lowering obey it; see (41).)

Returning to PRO, I suggest that it cannot occur in a Case-governed position. Though this does not exclude PRO from occurring in a governed position where no Case is assigned, it virtually gives the effect that PRO is ungoverned. M. Brody (1982) has argued that the fact that PRO is ungoverned can be derived from the Visibility Convention, together with the assumption that a non-Case-governed pronominal is interpreted as PRO. He thus challenges deriving the requirement concerning ungoverned PROs from the binding theory. Although of interest, this proposal is not directly relevant to our discussion.

3.5.2 Pronouns as Empty Categories

From the previous discussion of the distinction between PROs and pronouns, it is apparent that I am departing from the approach outlined in section 3.3 involving the functional characterization of empty categories. I am suggesting that *an empty element is interpreted as a pure pronominal, and not as PRO, if it is free or if it is locally bound by an element with an independent θ-role.* If this pronominal is inserted in a Case-governed context, it is interpreted as a nonanaphoric pronominal (i.e., as a pronoun); otherwise, it is interpreted as an anaphoric pronominal (i.e., as PRO). As a nonanaphoric pronominal, it will be subject to principle (B) of the binding theory only. As an anaphoric pronominal, it will be subject to principles (A) and (B); therefore, it must be ungoverned. Pronouns and PROs thus differ with respect to Case-government: pronouns, but not PROs, are Case-governed.

This approach has some far-reaching consequences. Now an empty element may be interpreted as a *wh*-trace if it is locally bound by an element in a nonargument position, as an NP-trace if it is locally bound by an element lacking an independent θ-role, and as a pronominal—not as PRO—if it is free or locally bound by an element with an independent θ-role. This pronominal is identified as a pronoun if it is Case-governed and as PRO if it is not Case-governed. In other words, *there is no type distinction between pronouns and empty categories:* pronouns are just a different occurrence of the "empty category" identified as such in terms of properties of the structures they appear in. Furthermore, since pronouns may be phonetically realized, there is no type distinction between the so-called null or nonovert elements (NP-trace, *wh*-trace, PRO) and nonnull pronouns (phonetically realized pronouns).

Consequently, the definition of anaphor adopted in chapter 2 and rewritten in (43) will have to be reformulated as shown in (44):

(43)
If α is an empty element, then it is an anaphor.

(44)
If α is an empty element, but not a *pronoun,* then it is an anaphor.

In section 2.2 we questioned the naturalness of definition (45)

(45)
If α is an empty element, but not *a variable,* then it is an anaphor.

and indicated that (43) no doubt represents an improvement. A priori, it seems that definition (44) is subject to the same criticism as (45): what natural classes does it single out?

Definition (44) singles out two classes: the first comprises PROs, NP-traces, and (phonetically unrealized) variables; the second, pronouns. In section 3.3 we assumed that an element with an incomplete matrix is an anaphor. It follows from this assumption that reflexives and reciprocals are anaphors, since they lack inherent reference. It also follows that PROs, NP-traces, and nonovert *wh*-traces are anaphors, since they do not satisfy the necessary conditions for phonetic realization. In brief, the first class singled out by definition (44) is natural. As opposed to the second class, all the members of this class share a common feature: they have an incomplete matrix. Actually, this discussion implies a stronger conclusion: definition (44) does not need to be stipulated as an independent definition; it follows from the assumption concerning anaphora discussed in section 3.3. Therefore, the naturalness of (44) does not come into question.

A desirable consequence of the view that there is no type distinction between pronouns and empty categories concerns the definition of variables. H. Koopman and D. Sportiche (1982) account for weak crossover effects by invoking the Bijection Principle, which states that there is a one-to-one relation between $\bar{\text{A}}$-binders and variables. Thus, consider (46):

(46)
*which girl$_i$ did her$_i$ mother beat x_i

Which girl locally $\bar{\text{A}}$-binds two variables, *her* and x, violating the Bijection Principle. As Koopman and Sportiche note, in order for this account to be maintained the definition of variables must be generalized to include pronouns:

(47)
α is a variable iff
a. α is an empty element or a pronoun
b. α is in an A-position
c. α is locally $\bar{\text{A}}$-bound.

Note that if there is no type distinction between pronouns and empty categories, the fact that pronouns can be interpreted as variables comes as no surprise. In fact, (47a) makes sense only if pronouns and empty categories are of the same type. But in that case (47) can be reformulated as follows:

(48)
α is a variable iff
a. α is an empty element
b. α is in an A-position
c. α is locally $\bar{\text{A}}$-bound.

In section 3.6.2 we will see that clause (48d) must be added to the definition:

(48)

d. α bears an independent θ-role.

3.5.3 Nonovert Anaphors in Chamorro

We have seen that definition (44) distinguishes two natural classes: the first contains PROs, NP-traces, and (phonetically unrealized) *wh*-traces; the second, pronouns. Pronouns differ from PROs with respect to Case-government: only pronouns are Case-governed. By virtue of not being Case-governed, PROs are anaphors:

(49)

a. Pronouns: [−anaphor, +pronominal]

b. PROs: [+anaphor, +pronominal]

The analysis presented here concerning the distinction between pronouns and PROs in terms of Case-government is incorporated into the theory of Chomsky 1982. As Chomsky notes, this analysis allows the parallelism between overt and empty categories to be maintained in its full generality. An element may be subject to either binding principle (A) or binding principle (B), to both of them, or to neither. This gives four possibilities:

(50)

a. [+anaphor, −pronominal]

b. [−anaphor, +pronominal]

c. [+anaphor, +pronominal]

d. [−anaphor, −pronominal]

In the case of overt categories, we find examples of (50a), (50b), and (50d): namely, overt anaphors (*each other*), pronouns (*he*), and R-expressions (*John*), respectively. As Chomsky points out, there could not be an overt element corresponding to (50c), since it would have to be ungoverned by virtue of being subject to binding principles (A) and (B). Being ungoverned, it would not receive Case, since Case is assigned under government, and it would therefore violate the Case Filter.

Assuming that the typology of empty elements mirrors that of overt categories, Chomsky indicates that unless some are barred by independent principles, we expect to find empty elements of each of the types (50a–d) and no others. In his terms, NP-trace fulfills type (50a), PRO type (50c), and *wh*-trace type (50d). As for type (50b), a nonovert pronominal anaphor satisfying only binding principle (B), Chomsky suggests that it is the empty element found in subject position in languages such as Italian, which allow a missing subject:

(51)
a. *e* parla
   'he is speaking'
b. *e* arriva un ragazzo
   'there arrives a boy'

Chomsky refers to this element as *pro*. Unlike PRO, pro can be governed, since it is subject only to binding principle (B); Chomsky cites as evidence Spanish examples from Torrego 1984. Moreover, assuming the distinction between pronominals made in terms of Case-government, he indicates that pro, contrary to PRO, is Case-marked. Actually, according to the distinction made in section 3.5.1 between Case-government and Case-marking, pro must be characterized as Case-governed. Thus, it is not an anaphor:

(52)
a. pros: [−anaphor, +pronominal]
b. PROs: [+anaphor, +pronominal]

From the parallelism between (49a–b) and (52a–b), it appears that pro is a Case-governed pronominal—i.e., a pronoun—that is not phonetically realized.

According to the characterization that an element is an anaphor if it lacks inherent reference or if it does not fulfill all the conditions for phonetic realization, pro is not an anaphor. It does fulfill the conditions for phonetic realization, and indeed it can be phonetically realized. The only specific requirement concerning pro is that it must be *identified*. As indicated in Aoun 1981a, pro may be identified if it is phonetically realized or if it is coindexed with a "rich enough" inflection; the latter case is the subject-drop parameter of Chomsky 1982. In other words, phonetic realization of pro and coindexation with a rich enough inflection are both instances of the same identification strategy.

In previous sections I have suggested that a Case-governed pronominal is interpreted as a pronoun. If we take the characterization of pro into account, this proposal means that a Case-governed pronominal is interpreted as a pronoun that may be identified by being phonetically realized or by a rich enough inflection. When the pronoun (i.e., the Case-governed pronominal) is not phonetically realized, it is referred to as pro. This means that the Case-governed pronominal generated by the LF process of Lowering is a pro. Note that in English this pro may be generated by LF rules but cannot be generated in Syntax, as illustrated by the ungrammaticality of *pro came. The ungrammaticality of this sentence is assumed to be due to the absence of a rich enough inflection in this language (Chomsky 1982). In brief, pro in English can be generated at LF but not in Syntax because in the latter instance the identification requirement would be violated. We may then conclude that this requirement applies in Syntax (or PF) but not at LF. In a sense this is not surprising. It has been suggested that the identification requirement is to be related to the principle of the recoverability of deletion. According to the organization of the grammar suggested in LGB, deletion rules apply at PF; thus, recoverability of deletion will be checked at PF. In case the identification requirement is to be related to (or subsumed under) recoverability of deletion, it will also apply at PF.

Another remark concerns *wh*-traces. According to Chomsky 1982, *wh*-traces are instances of (50d). We have seen here that they are instances of a special kind of anaphor ($\overline{\text{A}}$-anaphors) and that they are anaphors when they are not phonetically realized. In brief, when they are phonetically realized, *wh*-traces fulfill case (50d). When they are not phonetically realized, they fulfill case (50a): they are nonpronominal $\overline{\text{A}}$-anaphors subject to binding principle (A) and, as argued in chapter 2, to binding principle (C).

If we were to consider that *wh*-traces are not anaphoric, then, the nonovert anaphors would be NP-trace and PRO. However, I have stated that the nonovert anaphors are NP-trace, PRO, and *wh*-trace. The differences between the two characterizations are illustrated in (53):

(53)
Characterization of nonovert elements with respect to the features [±anaphor]
a. In an analysis where *wh*-traces are not anaphors
   [+anaphor]:   NP-trace, PRO
   [−anaphor]:   *wh*-trace, pro
b. In an analysis where *wh*-traces are anaphors
   [+anaphor]:   NP-trace, PRO, *wh*-trace
   [−anaphor]:   pro

One way of distinguishing between the two characterizations is to find a process that is triggered by nonovert anaphors. According to (53a), this process should be triggered by NP-traces and PROs; according to (53b), it should be triggered by NP-traces, PROs, and *wh*-traces. Such a process is found in Chamorro, and it seems to favor (53b) over (53a). (The Chamorro material discussed below is from a talk given at the University of Southern California by S. Chung in the fall of 1982. My thanks to S. Chung for fruitful discussions.)

In Chamorro, a Western Austronesian language, an inflection marker -*um* replaces the ergative agreement in realis constructions. This inflection marker occurs when the subject is raised, as illustrated in (54). (54a) indicates that 'begin' in Chamorro is a raising verb, and (54b) illustrates the occurrence of -*um* in raising constructions:

(54)
a. ha-tutuhun   umuchan
   INFL(3s)-begin rain
   'it began to rain'

b. ha-tutuhun   si   Miguel t-um-aitai i   lepblu
   INFL(3s)-begin UNM Miguel INFL-read the book
   'Miguel began to read the book'

The -*um* marker occurs when the subject is questioned. Sentences (55a) and (55b–c) are in the irrealis and realis moods, respectively:

(55)
a. hayi pära u-taitai   i   lepblu
   who will INFL(3s)-read the book
   'who is going to read the book'

b. *hayi ha-taitai   i   lepblu
   who INFL(3s)-read the book
   'who read the book'

c. *hayi t-um-aitai i   lepblu
   who INFL-read the book
   'who read the book'

The -*um* marker also occurs when the subject is relativized, as in (56a), or when it is focused, as in (56b):

(56)

a. i   taotao ni   t-um-aitai i   lepblu
the person COMP INFL-read the book
'the person who read the book'

b. guahu t-um-aitai i   lepblu
I   INFL-read the book
'I read the book'
(*I* is focused)

Finally, -*um* occurs with the subject of an infinitival clause, which is always nonovert, as illustrated by the ungrammaticality of (58b). The embedded clauses of (57a) and (58a) are tensed, and the embedded clauses of (57b) and (58b) are nontensed:

(57)

a. ma'a'ñao   yu' na   bai u-atsa   esti na kahun
INFL(s)-afraid I   COMP INFL(1s)-lift this   box
'I'm afraid that (= lest) I lift the box'

b. ma'a'ñao   yu' (*na)   um-atsa esti na kahun
INFL(s)-afraid I   COMP INFL-lift this   box
'I'm afraid to lift the box'

(58)

a. ma'a'ñao   yu' na   u-atsa   si   Mary esti na kahun
INFL(s)-afraid I   COMP INFL(3s)-lift UNM Mary this   box
'I'm afraid that (= lest) Mary lift this box'

b. *ma'a'ñao   yu' um-atsa si   Mary esti na kahun
INFL(s)-afraid I   INFL-lift UNM Mary this   box
'I'm afraid Mary to lift this box'

The -*um* marker does not occur when the subject is overt, however, as illustrated by the ungrammaticality of (59b). (59a–b) are to be contrasted with (59c), where the subject is focused.

(59)

a. ha-fa'tinas   i   patgun i   sena
INFL(3s)-make the child   the dinner
'the child made dinner'

b. *f-um-a'tinas   i   patgun i   sena
   INFL(3s)-make the child   the dinner
   'the child made dinner'

c. i   patgun f-um-a'tina i   sena
    the child   INFL-make the dinner
    'the child made dinner'
    (*the child* is focused)

Nor does the *-um* marker occur when the subject is dropped:

(60)

a. ha-taitai   i   lepblu
    INFL(3s)-read the book
    'he read the book'

b. *t-um-aitai   i   lepblu
    INFL-read the book
    'he read the book'

In brief, assuming that focus involves *Wh*-Movement (Chomsky 1977b),
it appears that *-um* occurs with NP-traces, *wh*-traces, and PROs but
not with pros and lexical subjects. If we were to assume that *wh*-traces
are not anaphors, as in (53a), we would be forced to claim that *-um*
occurs with nonovert anaphors (NP-trace, PRO) and *wh*-trace, elements that surely do not form a natural class. On the other hand,
characterization (53b) raises no such problem. The generalization is
quite obvious: *-um* appears with nonovert anaphors (NP-trace, PRO,
and *wh*-trace). Insofar as this generalization is more naturally expressed in an approach that incorporates the notion of $\overline{\text{A}}$-anaphor, it
provides further evidence for this approach.

3.6 The Interpretation of Empty Elements

3.6.1 The Interpretation of NP-Traces
In section 3.1.3 I noted that the (non)referential status of the nonovert
pronominal element generated by Lowering need not be stipulated; it
follows from the Projection Principle. This approach may be extended
to other occurrences of empty elements. Consider first NP-traces. Two
constructions are relevant: those where the antecedent of the NP-trace
is not an argument, as in (61a), and those where it is, as in (61b):

(61)

a. NP   t
   non-R-expression
   (Example: it seems to be certain that John left)

b. NP   t
   R-expression
   (Example: John was killed)

The trace and its antecedent are in the same chain. In (61b) the trace cannot be interpreted as an R-expression; if it is, the chain will contain two R-expressions. Nor can it be an R-expression in (61a). Two possibilities arise: (a) the antecedent is in a θ-position, and (b) the trace is in a θ-position. Both (a) and (b) are excluded by the Projection Principle: if the antecedent were in a θ-position, this θ-position would have been empty prior to movement; if the trace were in a θ-position, this θ-position would have been occupied by a non-R-expression prior to movement. In neither case would the θ-Criterion have been satisfied at D-structure, thus violating the Projection Principle. Since in (61a) neither the trace nor its antecedent may be in a θ-position, the chain containing this trace will not receive a θ-role; therefore, the representation will be excluded by the θ-Criterion.

In brief, the only grammatical representation is the one where the NP-trace is treated as a non-R-expression:

(62)

a. NP ...   t
   non-R-expression   non-R-expression

b. NP ...   t
   R-expression   non-R-expression

3.6.2 The Interpretation of Variables

Let us now consider variables bound by a *wh*-operator:

(63)

$wh_i \ldots x_i$

We have been assuming that the variable is an R-expression (a namelike element): as an empty element it will be subject to binding principle (A) and as an R-expression to binding principle (C).

As indicated in LGB (chapter 6), the fact that variables are R-expressions (or more generally arguments) accounts for the ungrammaticality of sentences such as (64) where the *wh*-trace is not assigned a referential value:

(64)
*what$_i$ x_i rains

The traces considered so far are $\overline{\text{A}}$-bound by a *wh*-operator. At this point, it is possible to consider that variables are inherently treated as arguments or that they are arguments by virtue of being coindexed with a *wh*-operator. For concreteness, if the second option were taken, it would be possible to assume that [+wh] is among the features copied by Move α onto the empty element when a *wh*-quantifier is extracted. The two approaches are different. The first considers that all instances of variables are arguments. The second considers that a variable is an argument only when it is coindexed with a *wh*-operator; it amounts to saying that only potentially referential expressions may be questioned. This approach allows the existence of nonargument variables, that is, empty elements $\overline{\text{A}}$-bound by a nonoperator. Such variables do appear to exist.

In section 2.6.1 I indicated that clitics are in an $\overline{\text{A}}$-position and that they may bind the variable left by the extraction of *wh*-elements. Obviously, clitics are not operators. Thus, clitics illustrate a clear case where an $\overline{\text{A}}$-binder is not an operator. With this in mind, consider the following representation:

(65)
Pierre le$_i$ voit e_i
'Pierre sees him'

Since clitics are in an $\overline{\text{A}}$-position, the empty element coindexed with the clitic is identified as a variable.

There are reasons to believe that this variable is not treated as an argument (i.e., that it does not have a referential value): it does not bear a θ-role. Consider (66):

(66)
e_i il$_i$ est difficile de partir
'it is difficult to leave'

Since clitics are in an $\overline{\text{A}}$-position, the empty element left by the cliticization of the subject is identified as a variable. This variable cannot be an argument: either it is in the same chain with the clausal argument *de partir* or it is not. In the first case, two arguments will be in the same chain; in the second, the chain containing the variable will not be in a θ-position or, alternatively, *de partir* will not have a θ-role. In brief, the variable coindexed with the clitic does not bear a θ-role by itself; it cannot be an argument. It has been suggested, however, that subject clitics, unlike other clitics, are generated in PF and not in Syntax. If this turns out to be correct, then the conclusion based on (66) cannot be maintained.

However, other considerations suggest that the clitic, and not the variable coindexed with the clitic, may have a referential value and thus may bear a θ-role. These considerations involve coreference facts discussed in Rizzi 1982b, although my conclusion will be slightly different from the one advocated there. Rizzi notes the following contrast in Italian:

(67)
a. Gianni ha mandato [$_{NP}$ la sorella di Piero$_i$] [$_{PP}$ incontro a lui$_i$]
   Gianni sent   the sister of Piero   towards to him

b. Gianni gli$_i$ ha mandato [$_{NP}$ la sorella di Piero] [incontro e_i]
   Gianni to him sent   the sister of Piero   towards
   'Gianni sent Piero's sister to meet him'

In (67a) *Piero* and the pronoun *lui* may be understood as coreferential. In (67b), however, the dative clitic *gli* and *Piero* may not be. These facts may be interpreted as follows. Let us assume that coreference relations may hold only between elements bearing a θ-role. According to the θ-Criterion, only arguments (such as R-expressions) bear a θ-role. In (67a) the R-expressions *Piero* and *lui* may be understood as coreferential. In (67b), however, assuming that the clitic and not the empty element bears a θ-role, coreference between *gli* and *Piero* will be excluded by considerations along the lines of principle (C) of the binding theory (see Chomsky 1982): *Piero* will be coreferential with a c-commanding element bearing a θ-role. Assuming, however, that the empty element and not the clitic bears a θ-role, we would incorrectly predict that (67a) and (67b) should be treated alike.

The following facts in Spanish corroborate this analysis:

(68)
a. le presentamos [la admiradora de Juan]
b. le$_i$ presentamos [la admiradora de Juan] a el$_i$
   'we presented the admirer of Juan to him'

In (68b), but not in (68a), the dative clitic *le* cooccurs with a doubled pronoun, *a el*. In (68a) coreference between the clitic and *Juan* is not possible. In (68b) coreference between *Juan* and the chain (*le, a el*) is possible. The impossibility of coreference between the clitic and *Juan* in (68a) is parallel to the situation found in (67b). As for (68b), I have argued in Aoun 1981b that in doubled constructions such as (68b), the dative clitic is not an R-expression and does not have a θ-role; rather, it is the doubled element *a el* that bears a θ-role. Since coreference relations hold between R-expressions only, it follows that in (68b) the coreference relation holds between the doubled pronoun *a el* and the NP *Juan* and not between the doubling clitic *le* and this NP. In other words, (68b) is to be treated like (67a) and not like (67b).

In brief, the coreference facts illustrated in (67) and (68) indicate that in nondoubled constructions the clitic—and not the empty element coindexed with it—bears a θ-role. The variable coindexed with the clitic cannot be an argument. If correct, this result may have some important consequences for the application of the binding principles. Recall that variables are subject as anaphors to binding principle (A) and as arguments (namelike elements) to binding principle (C). It is interesting to wonder whether both principles apply to variables that are not arguments—that is, to clitic-traces.

As formulated, binding principle (C) applies to names and namelike expressions (which are arguments). Since some variables are nonarguments, we may expect them not to be subject to this principle. If so, nonargument variables will be subject to principle (A) only: they will have to be $\bar{\text{A}}$-bound in their governing category. Moreover, recall from chapter 2 that neither AGR nor [NP,S] can count as an accessible SUBJECT for variables in nonsubject position; this was excluded by the fact that variables are subject to binding principle (C). Suppose now that nonargument variables are not subject to principle (C). Then nothing prevents AGR or [NP,S] from counting as an accessible SUB-JECT for these variables when they occur in nonsubject position. In other words, the governing category for these variables will be the same as the governing category for NP-traces occurring in the same position. The difference between these variables and NP-traces will be that the former must be $\bar{\text{A}}$-bound and the latter A-bound in this governing category. This is precisely the case for variables $\bar{\text{A}}$-bound by clitics: they are subject only to binding principle (A).

To see the distinction between argument and nonargument variables, consider the following two structures:

(69)

a. $[_{\bar{S}_1}$ what$_i$ $[_{S_1}$ do you want $[_{\bar{S}_0}[_{S_0}$ PRO to eat $x_i]]]]$

b. $[_{\bar{S}_1}[_{S_1}$ je veux $[_{\bar{S}_0}[_{S_0}$ PRO l$_i$'acheter $x_i]]]]$

      I want   it to buy

     'I want to buy it'

In (69a) neither PRO nor the AGR element of the matrix clause counts as an accessible SUBJECT for the variable because this variable would be potentially A-bound by the subject of S_0 or S_1. Thus, this variable, which is governed by the embedded verb *eat*, has no accessible SUBJECT, and the main clause counts as the governing category.

In (69b), however, assuming that nonargument variables are not subject to binding principle (C), nothing prevents PRO from counting as accessible SUBJECT for this variable. The governing category for this variable will be the embedded $\bar{S}$, since it is the minimal category containing a governor V and an accessible SUBJECT.

In brief, the domains in which the argument variable in (69a) and the nonargument variable in (69b) must be $\bar{A}$-bound are the main clause and the embedded clause, respectively. To present the matter differently, only the variable in (69b) is subject to the Specified Subject Condition (SSC): it must be $\bar{A}$-bound in the domain delimited by the subject of the clause in which it appears.

As pointed out in Kayne 1975, the distribution of clitics in French follows from the SSC:

(70)

a. elle voudrait   [PRO le$_i$ manger e_i]

    she would like   it eat

    'she would like to eat it'

b. je croyais [PRO la$_i$ connaître e_i]

    I thought   her to know

    'I thought I knew her'

c. elle a laissé [Jean lui$_i$ offrir un livre e_i]

    she let   Jean to her offer a   book

    'she let Jean offer her a book'

(71)

a. *elle le$_i$ voudrait [PRO manger e_i]

b. *je la$_i$ croyais [PRO connaître e_i]

c. *elle lui$_i$ a laissé [Jean lui offrir un livre e_i]

The SSC correctly accounts for the ungrammaticality of (71a–c), since in these sentences the clitic has been extracted from the domain of its subject. In terms of the binding principles, the governing category for the empty element coindexed with the clitic in (71a–c) is the embedded clause. In this governing category the empty element is free, thus violating principle (A) of the binding theory.

It is possible, then, to distinguish two kinds of $\overline{A}$-bound empty elements: those that are arguments and those that are not. The former are coindexed with a *wh*-quantifier, the latter with a clitic. As anaphors, the two kinds of empty elements will be subject to principle (A) of the binding theory. However, only empty elements coindexed with a *wh*-quantifier are arguments and thereby subject to principle (C); moreover, only these elements are not subject to the SSC. For ease of exposition, I will refer to empty elements coindexed with a *wh*-element as *wh-traces* or *variables* and to empty elements coindexed with a clitic as *clitic-traces*. In section 5.3 I will discuss other instances of $\overline{A}$-bound empty elements that are not arguments.

3.7 Domains of Application of the Binding Principles

We have seen that the ECP may be dispensed with if the binding theory is generalized to a theory of X-binding. Since the ECP is assumed to apply at LF, the binding principles must apply at LF too, though this obviously does not mean they cannot apply elsewhere. In fact, there is evidence that they also apply at S-structure.

The evidence that the binding principles apply at LF includes the fact that the output of the LF Lowering process is constrained by the binding theory (section 3.1); constructions involving extraction of *wh*-elements from inside an NP in Romance (section 2.6) and Hebrew (section 2.6.1); and violations of the Superiority Condition (section 2.7.1).

Let us briefly recapitulate one of these constructions. Recall that in French the subject of an NP, but not its object, may be extracted by *Wh*-Movement:

(72)
a.   tu as vu [$_{NP}$ le portrait d'Aristote de Rembrandt]
                            obj   subj
b.   l'artiste dont$_i$ tu as vu [$_{NP}$ le portrait d'Aristote x_i]
c.   *l'homme dont$_i$ tu as vu [$_{NP}$ le portrait x_i de Rembrandt]

This contrast is accounted for by the binding theory: in (72b–c) the governing category is the NP. In this category, the variable of (72b), but not that of (72c), is $\bar{\text{A}}$-bound by the determiner. A similar contrast holds when the *wh*-elements have not been moved in Syntax:

(73)
a. tu as vu [$_{NP}$ le portrait d'Aristote de quel artiste]
b. *tu as vu [$_{NP}$ le portrait de quel homme de Rembrandt]

By assuming that *Wh*-Raising, which applies in LF, raises these *wh*-elements and adjoins them outside the NP, the respective LF representations of (73a–b) will be similar to those of (72b–c). The ungrammaticality of (73b) will be treated like that of (72c): both involve a violation of the binding theory. Once again, this account provides evidence for the LF nature of the binding theory, since an LF movement rule, *Wh*-Raising, is constrained by this theory.

The evidence suggesting that the binding theory applies at S-structure essentially involves what have been called *parasitic gaps* (Taraldsen 1981, Engdahl 1983). The evidence to be presented here is based on Chomsky 1982.

Parasitic gaps are constructions in which two empty elements are related to a single operator:

(74)
a. which articles did John file e_1 without reading e_2
b. this is the kind of food you must cook e_1 before you eat e_2

Following Chomsky 1982, I will refer to e_1 as the *licensing variable* and to e_2 as the *parasitic gap*. Parasitic gaps have specific properties that need not concern us here (but see the above-mentioned references). For our purposes, it suffices to note that the licensing variable must be present at S-structure, as illustrated in (75):

(75)
a. which book did you file e_1 without reading e_2
b. *I forgot who filed which book without reading e

This contrast may be accounted for by assuming that the binding theory applies at S-structure. At this level, the quantifier *which book* in (75b) has not yet undergone *Wh*-Raising; the empty element e is free and is thus interpreted as a pronominal. This pronominal is in a Case-governed context; if we choose to assign Case, it will be interpreted as a pronoun and phonetically realized in PF, and there will no longer be a parasitic gap:

(76)

I forgot who filed which book without reading it

If we choose not to assign Case, however, this pronominal will be interpreted as PRO, as in (75b). Since this PRO is in a governed context, the derivation will be filtered out by the binding theory. (75a) does not violate the binding theory because the parasitic gap is interpreted as a variable bound by the operator *which book*. As indicated above, this account crucially assumes that the binding theory applies at S-structure. Were the binding principles to apply only at LF, (75a–b) would essentially have similar LF representations after the application of LF movement rules, and the binding theory would not draw the correct distinction between the two sentences.

In sum, there is evidence both that the binding theory applies at LF (after the application of LF movement rules) and that it applies at S-structure (before LF movement rules). Therefore, let us assume that the binding principles in fact apply at both levels, S-structure and LF (after LF movement rules). Note that we do not want the binding principles to apply at D-structure because many constructions involve a violation of these principles at this level:

(77)

a. I want [PRO$_i$ to be kissed t_i]   (at S-structure)

b. I want [e_1 to be kissed e_2]   (at D-structure)
   (at D-structure e_2 is interpreted as PRO: this PRO is in a governed context)

Nor do we want the binding principles to apply at PF—across languages, PF rules such as scrambling rules do not seem to obey them. Thus, the binding principles apply at LF and S-structure only. In a sense, though, this is not suprising. There are two components in the grammar where the various anaphoric processes may be determined: Syntax and LF. In Syntax they may be determined by Move α and (free) indexing, which applies at S-structure. In LF they may be determined by LF movement rules and (free) indexing, which may apply here as well. In other words, syntactic and LF movement rules, as well as the indexing mechanism, create anaphoric relations. The binding principles may be thought of as well-formedness principles checking the various anaphoric relations; they determine which anaphoric relations may (or must) hold and which may not. It is therefore natural that the binding principles apply at the output of each component where anaphoric relations are determined—that is, at S-structure and at LF (by definition, PF rules do not affect anaphoric relations). This does not mean that this fact is logically necessary: the above remarks are consistent with a grammar in which anaphoric relations are checked only when all anaphoric relations are determined—that is, at LF.

The assumption that the binding principles apply at S-structure and at LF does not affect the conclusion that there is no pied-piping at LF (section 2.8.3). The central motivation for not assuming that pied-piping exists at LF concerned the following French sentences (= (139a–b) of chapter 2):

(78)
a. *il_i a aimé quels livres que Jean$_i$ a lus
b. quels livres que Jean$_i$ a lus a-t-il$_i$ aimés
   'which books that Jean read did he like'

In (78b), but not in (78a), intended coreference between *il* and *Jean* is possible. This contrast is accounted for by assuming that pied-piping does not apply at LF. As a result, *il* will always c-command *Jean* and the binding principles will prevent *Jean* and *il* from being coindexed. In (78b), however, nothing prevents the two elements from being coreferential, since *il* does not c-command *Jean*. Under the assumption that the binding principles apply at S-structure and at LF, this result carries over. Let us assume that indexing may freely apply at S-structure and at LF—that is, that any element, whether in A- or in Ā-position, may be freely coindexed with another element. Suppose now that pied-piping applies optionally in LF. Consider (78a). At S-structure we may choose not to coindex *il* and *Jean;* the binding theory will be irrelevant. At LF, if pied-piping applies, (78a) will essentially have a representation similar to (78b). Nothing would prevent *il* and *Jean* from being coindexed—an undesirable result. Suppose, however, that pied-piping may not apply in LF. At S-structure we may again choose not to coindex *il* and *Jean;* the binding theory will again be irrelevant. At LF, since pied-piping may not apply, we will not be able to coindex *il* and *Jean* because the representation will be excluded by the binding theory: *Jean* will be A-bound by the chain containing *il.* In brief, if we assume that pied-piping does not apply in LF, we can correctly account for the ungrammaticality of (78a); with the opposite assumption, we cannot. Since the assumption that pied-piping does not apply in LF carries over if the binding principles are checked at S-structure and at LF, the conclusions based on this assumption (for instance, that preposition stranding is not to be accounted for by the ECP) are not affected (see section 2.8.3).

Though we have crucially assumed that indexing applies freely at S-structure and LF, I would now like to explore another possibility. N. Chomsky (1982) suggests that at S-structure, indexing is to be restricted to A-indexing: that is, that only elements in A-positions may be coindexed. The reason for this essentially involves the behavior of pronouns in parasitic gap constructions. As indicated above, parasitic gaps may be licensed by a variable. Phonetically realized pronouns, however, do not license parasitic gaps:

(79)
a. *a man whom everyone who meets *him* knows someone who admires *e*
b. *a man whom everyone who meets *e* knows someone who admires *him*

Since they are contained in relative clauses, both italicized positions in (79a–b) are inaccessible to syntactic movement: the putative movement will involve a violation of Subjacency. Now suppose that indexing, at S-structure, is not restricted to A-positions—that is, that all elements, whether in A- or in $\bar{\text{A}}$-positions, may be freely coindexed. Nothing would prevent *him* and *e* in (79) from being coindexed with *whom;* both *him* and *e* will be interpreted as variables $\bar{\text{A}}$-bound by *whom.* Consequently, (79a–b) should be treated like other constructions involving parasitic gaps. This is not the case: parasitic gaps are marginal (see (74)), whereas (79a–b) are completely ungrammatical.

Suppose, however, that indexing at S-structure is restricted to elements in A-position. We will then have a means to distinguish constructions like (79a–b) from parasitic gap constructions: in (79a–b) the empty element *e* will be free, hence interpreted as PRO. Since this PRO is in a governed position, the constructions will be excluded by the binding principles.

As indicated in Chomsky 1982, however, one shortcoming of this approach is that it predicts that (73a–b) ought to be treated like (79a–b). That is, it predicts that they ought to be excluded for the same reasons excluding (79a–b): both empty elements in (80) will be free, hence interpreted as PROs. These PROs being in governed positions, (80) should be excluded by the binding principles:

(80)

?a man whom everyone who meets *e* knows someone who admires *e*

Unfortunately, (80) seems to be better than (79a–b). Despite these remarks, let us assume that indexing at S-structure is restricted to A-indexing. Furthermore, let us assume that at LF the opposite holds— in other words, that at LF the relevant indexing is $\bar{A}$-indexing: elements in A- or $\bar{A}$-positions may only be indexed with elements in $\bar{A}$-position. With this in mind, let us return to (78a). At S-structure, if *il* and *Jean* are coindexed, the derivation will be excluded by the binding theory. Suppose, however, we choose not to index *il* and *Jean* at S-structure. Since clitics are in $\bar{A}$-position, we will be able to coindex *il* and *Jean* at LF, and the results will again be ruled out along the lines of binding principle (C) (see Chomsky 1982): *Jean* will be c-commanded by the chain containing the clitic *il* and the trace of this clitic, which is in A-position. It has been suggested, however, that subject clitics are generated in PF (see the discussion below (66)). Let us assume for the sake of the argument that this is so. In Syntax and LF, *il* is still in A-position like *Jean*. If indexing at LF is restricted to $\bar{A}$-indexing, we will account correctly for the fact that *il* and *Jean* in (78a) cannot be coreferential: since they are in A-positions, it will not be possible to coindex them at LF. In brief, either *il* and *Jean* are coindexed at S-structure in violation of the binding theory, or they cannot be co-indexed at all. Under the assumption that $\bar{A}$-indexing is restricted to LF, there will be no well-formed representation where these elements are coindexed; thus, they cannot be interpreted as coreferential. Under this analysis, we no longer need to maintain that pied-piping may not apply at LF. If this is so, the conclusion based on the assumption that pied-piping may not apply at LF will have to be reconsidered and treated along the lines suggested at the end of section 2.8.3.

3.8 Summary

We began this chapter by studying a particular instance of "Move α" in LF and have argued as follows:

a. There exists a process of Lowering in LF applying to quantifiers and to pleonastic elements such as *there* (sections 3.1.1 and 3.1.2).

b. It follows from the Projection Principle that chains constitute the domain in which Lowering applies: the antecedent of a trace may be lowered to the position occupied by the trace. The controller of

PRO, however, may not be lowered to the position occupied by PRO (section 3.1.3).

c. The output of these lowering processes is subject to the binding principles, thus providing further evidence for the LF nature of these principles (section 3.1.2).

d. These lowering processes are made possible by the existence of a general LF process inserting a nonreferential PRO in Case-governed contexts (section 3.2).

e. If it is assumed that pronouns are always generated as a set of features [αperson, βnumber, γgender] and that they are phonetically realized in PF when they are Case-governed, then the output of the nonovert pronominal insertion process that occurs in Case-governed contexts is not filtered out by the binding theory: only non-Case-governed pronominals (PROs) must be ungoverned (sections 3.2 and 3.3).

f. Whether overt or not, this insertion process—like other insertion processes affecting pronominal elements—can be eliminated in favor of more interpretive principles. As a result, the various contextual restrictions governing this insertion mechanism do not need to be stipulated: they derive from the grammatical principles (such as the binding theory) already at work in the grammar (section 3.4).

g. These proposals entail a reinterpretation of the notion "empty category": pronouns are simply a different occurrence of the empty category identified as such in terms of properties of the structure they appear in. In other words, there is no type distinction between pronouns and the other empty categories (NP-traces, *wh*-traces, PROs) (section 3.5).

h. Pursuing the identification of the various occurrences of the empty category, two kinds of $\overline{\text{A}}$-bound nonovert elements can be distinguished: *wh*-traces (variables coindexed with a *wh*-operator in $\overline{\text{A}}$-position) and clitic-traces (more generally, nonovert elements coindexed with a nonoperator in $\overline{\text{A}}$-position). These two kinds of nonovert empty elements behave differently with respect to the binding principles. As anaphors, both are subject to binding principle (A). As arguments, however, only *wh*-traces are subject to principle (C). Being subject to principles (A) and (C), *wh*-traces escape the effect of the so-called Specified Subject Condition (SSC). Empty elements $\overline{\text{A}}$-bound by nonoperators, such as clitics, are subject only to principle (A) and therefore obey the SSC (section 3.6).

i. Lowering processes as well as other LF rules studied in chapter 2 appear to be constrained by the binding theory, which therefore must apply at LF. Other evidence indicates that the binding theory also applies at S-structure. More generally, the binding principles apply at the output of each component where anaphoric relations are determined, namely, at S-structure and at LF (section 3.7).

Chapter 4
Argument Structure

In chapter 3 we briefly considered an instance of a nonovert $\overline{\text{A}}$-anaphor (clitic-trace) that does not bear an independent θ-role. Here we will study this element in more detail through its distribution in French causative constructions. This study will bear on the characterization of crucial notions at work in the theory of binding. It will be suggested that

a. the notion *accessible SUBJECT* in terms of which governing categories are defined is to be replaced by that of *accessible chains;*

b. argument structures are relevant to the characterization of opaque domains: SUBJECTs (or chains containing SUBJECTs) are accessible to elements that belong to the same argument structure;

c. the relevant notion of chain in the grammar is thematic chain (θ-chain) and not A-chain or $\overline{\text{A}}$-chain.

4.1 Causatives in French

Among the constructions given in chapter 3 to illustrate the fact that clitic-traces obey the Specified Subject Condition (SSC) were causative constructions involving the verb *laisser* 'to let' (see section 3.6.2). As illustrated in (1) and (2), *laisser* can be followed by a lexical subject, but *faire* 'to have/make someone do something' cannot:[1]

(1)
Marie a laissé Paul partir
'Marie let Paul leave'

(2)
*Jean a fait Marie partir
 'Jean had Marie leave'

With both *faire* and *laisser,* the subject of the embedded sentence can appear to the right of the infinitive:

(3)
on a fait sortir Marie du bureau
'they had Marie leave the office'

(4)
Marie a laissé partir Paul
'Marie let Paul leave'

The derivation of these structures involves the application of a transformation—$\overline{V}$-Preposing—that moves the embedded verbal constituent to the front of the clause. The rule operates as follows, starting with a base structure like (5):

(5)
on a fait [Marie [$_{\overline{V}}$[$_{\overline{V}}$[$_V$ sortir]] du bureau]]

$\overline{V}$-Preposing may then front the verb:

(6)
on a fait [sortir Marie $\overline{V}$ du bureau]
($\overline{V}$ is the trace of *sortir*)

Examples (1) through (6) involve intransitive infinitives. When the infinitive takes a direct object, the underlying subject appears after the object complement preceded by *à,* as in (7b), derived from (7a) (for further details, see Kayne 1975 and SRS):

(7)
a. Marie fera [Jean lire ce livre]
b. Marie fera lire ce livre à Jean
   'Marie will make Jean read that book'

The insertion of *à* does not need to be stipulated. It has been suggested that a general property of causatives assigns the grammatical function (in)direct object to the subject of a clausal complement (Aissen and Perlmutter 1976, Postal 1977). In French, when $\overline{V}$-Preposing occurs, the subject of the clausal complement is assigned the grammatical function indirect object in the presence of a direct object; otherwise, it is assigned the grammatical function direct object, as evidenced by the cliticization of this subject (Bordelois 1974):

(8)

a. j'ai fait manger la pomme à Jean

                                IO

   I made eat   the apple to Jean

   'I made Jean eat the apple'

b. je lui ai fait manger la pomme

   IO

   I him made eat   the apple

   'I made him eat the apple'

(9)

a. j'ai fait manger Jean

                     DO

   I made eat   Jean

   'I made Jean eat'

b. je l'ai fait   manger

   DO

   I him made eat

   'I made him eat'

In other words, suppose we assume that in French the primary object is the direct object and the secondary object is the indirect object. In causative constructions, when $\overline{V}$-Preposing occurs, the subject becomes a dependent of (is governed by) the fronted $\overline{V}$ (see SRS) and must look for a grammatical function: if the primary object is taken, as in (8), it assumes the secondary one. The secondary object in French is of the form *à NP*. Consequently, when a subject assumes the grammatical function of secondary object, the Case-marker *à* is inserted in front of its subject. This may be taken as the insight behind the *à*-insertion rule of SRS. This account does not mean that the *à*-insertion rule is not subject to further conditions; see SRS for discussion of such conditions and Williams 1981b for the suggestion that the *à*-insertion rule may be affected by considerations such as the thematic roles assigned to the elements in the clause embedded under the causative verb. I am implicitly assuming that two elements in the same clause may not take the same grammatical function. This is reminiscent of such well-formedness conditions as the θ-Criterion (two elements in the same clause may not assume the same θ-role) and the Biuniqueness Principle (two elements in the same clause may not have the same Case

(Vergnaud (forthcoming))); see Aoun 1979 for an attempt to subsume these two well-formedness conditions under a more general one.

Of course, the fact that (for instance) two $à + NPs$ occur in the same clause, as in (10), does not mean that they have the same Case. As evidenced by their corresponding clitics in (11a) and (11b), *à une symphonie* and *à Paul* have different Case:

(10)
Jean a fait comparer cette sonatine à Paul à une symphonie
'Jean had Paul compare that sonata with a symphony'

(11)
a. Jean fera y comparer cette sonatine à Paul
   'Jean will have Paul compare that sonata with it'

b. Jean lui fera comparer cette sonatine à une symphonie
   'Jean will have him compare that sonata with a symphony'

Notice that $\overline{V}$-Preposing affects only the verb and the direct object (the "small VP" in the sense of Williams 1974) but not the other complements. (12) is to be contrasted with (6) (repeated here):

(12)
*on a fait [sortir du bureau Marie $\overline{\overline{V}}$]
($\overline{\overline{V}}$ is the trace of *sortir du bureau*)

(6)
on a fait [sortir Marie $\overline{V}$ du bureau]
($\overline{V}$ is the trace of *sortir*)

After a verb like *faire,* $\overline{V}$-Preposing is obligatory; after a verb like *laisser,* it is optional. Here too, the obligatory application of the rule does not need to be stipulated. In *laisser* constructions, the embedded subject can receive a Case-feature directly from *laisser* (*laisser* thus triggers $\overline{S}$-Deletion and assigns Case to the embedded subject) or via $\overline{V}$-Preposing (as indicated by *à*-insertion, which is characteristic of $\overline{V}$-Preposing):

(13)
a. j'ai laissé Paul acheter un gâteau
   'I let Paul buy a cake'

b. j'ai laissé acheter un gâteau à Paul
   'I let Paul buy a cake'

On the other hand, in *faire* constructions the subject cannot receive a Case-feature directly from *faire*. Consequently, $\overline{V}$-Preposing must apply in order for the embedded subject to receive Case. Finally, it is irrelevant for the purpose of the following discussions whether the preposed $\overline{V}$ is base-generated or derived by a movement rule as assumed in SRS:

(14)
a. *Jean a fait Marie partir
b. Jean a fait partir Marie

4.2 Accessible Subjects versus Accessible Chains

We have been examining causative constructions because of their relevance to the application of the SSC. In causative constructions the subject defines a domain in which cliticization may occur. Our examples have involved causative constructions where $\overline{V}$-Preposing does not apply—that is, where the subject of the embedded clausal complement receives its Case from the matrix verb *laisser:*

(15)
a. Marie a laissé Paul lire ces romans
   'Marie let Paul read these novels'
b. Marie a laissé Paul les$_i$ lire x_i ·
   'Marie let Paul read them'
c. *Marie les$_i$ a laissé Paul lire x_i

As indicated in Kayne 1975 and SRS, the SSC still holds when $\overline{V}$-Preposing applies (in the following examples, x is the trace of the prepositional clitic y, and $\overline{V}$ is the trace of the moved verbal constituent):

(16)
a. Jean fera   [comparer cette sonatine à Paul à   une symphonie
   Jean will make compare that sonata   to Paul with a   symphony
   'Jean will have Paul compare that sonata with a symphony'
b. Jean fera [y$_i$ comparer cette sonatine à Paul $\overline{V}$ x_i]
                with it
   'Jean will have Paul compare that sonata with it'
c. *Jean y$_i$ fera [comparer cette sonatine à Paul $\overline{V}$ x_i]
   'Jean will have Paul compare that sonata with it'

(17)
a. Jean fera   [mettre ce   livre à   Pierre sur l'étagère]
    Jean will make put   that book to Pierre on the shelf
    'Jean will have Pierre put that book on the shelf'
b. Jean fera [y_i mettre ce livre à Pierre $\overline{\text{V}}$ x_i]
              on it
    'Jean will have Pierre put that book on it'
c. *Jean y_i fera [mettre ce livre à Pierre $\overline{\text{V}}$ x_i]
    'Jean will have Pierre put that book on it'

Paradigm (16)–(17) is parallel to the one exemplified in (15). The (c)
sentences illustrate an SSC violation: the trace of the clitic has its
antecedent outside the domain delimited by the embedded subject (*à
Paul* and *à Pierre*). This opaque domain is the embedded clause. The
embedded clause contains a governor—the verb—and an accessible
SUBJECT for the trace of the clitic. The embedded clause is therefore
the governing category for this trace.

   Surprisingly enough, as indicated in SRS section 6, when the embedded subject is itself cliticized in the (c) sentences, these sentences become grammatical (in the following examples, x is the trace of the
prepositional clitic y, x' the trace of the cliticized subject, and $\overline{V}$ the
trace of the moved verbal constituent). (16d) and (17d) are to be contrasted with (16c) and (17c), respectively:

(16)
d. Jean leur y_i fera [comparer cette sonatine x' $\overline{\text{V}}$ x_i]
            to them with it
    'Jean will have them compare that sonata with it'

(17)
d. Jean leur y_i fera [mettre ce livre x' $\overline{\text{V}}$ x_i]
            to them on it
    'Jean will have them put that book on it'

   The generalization that emerges from the paradigm (16)–(17) is that a
prepositional clitic originating in the lower clause cannot be adjoined to
the causative verb if the embedded subject is not itself cliticized onto
this causative verb. In terms of the framework adopted in chapter 3,
when the embedded subject in a causative construction is not cliticized,
the embedded clause functions as the governing category for the trace
left by the prepositional clitic. However, when the embedded subject is

cliticized, it seems that the matrix clause functions as the governing category for this trace (but see below): it is as if the cliticized subject—and not the empty element left by cliticization—functions as (an accessible) SUBJECT.

The notion "SUBJECT" assumed so far includes the subject of an infinitive, the subject of an NP, and AGR but not the subject of a tensed clause (SUBJECTs are italicized):

(18)

a. NP *AGR* V... (where the sentence is finite, as in "John *AGR* saw Bill")

b. *NP* V (where the sentence is nonfinite, like the embedded clause in "John wants *PRO* to go")

Intuitively, the notion SUBJECT characterizes the most prominent element in a given configuration. The cliticization facts illustrated above indicate that the chain constituted by the cliticized subject *and* its trace—rather than the trace left in subject position—functions as (an accessible) SUBJECT. Let us therefore replace the notion "accessible SUBJECT" by the notion "accessible chain":

(19)

A chain α is *accessible* to an element β iff α contains a SUBJECT accessible to β.

The definition of accessibility will be kept as it is, and the definition of governing category (20) will be modified as in (21) to refer to "accessible chain" instead of "accessible SUBJECT":

(20)

β is a *governing category* for α iff β is the minimal maximal projection containing α, a governor of α, and a SUBJECT accessible to α (= (49) of chapter 2).

(21)

β is a *governing category* for α iff β is the minimal maximal projection containing α, a governor of α, and a chain accessible to α.

For example, consider sentences such as (17c–d) (repeated here):

(17)

c. *Jean y_i fera [mettre ce livre à Pierre $\overline{V}$ x_i]

d. Jean leur y_i fera [mettre ce livre x' $\overline{V}$ x_i]

In (17c) the governing category for the trace x_i of y is the embedded clause; it is the minimal maximal projection containing an accessible chain (*à Pierre*) and a governor (*mettre*). This trace is free in its governing category, thus violating the binding principles. In (17d), however, the minimal maximal projection containing an accessible chain (*leur, x'*) and a governor for the trace x_i is the matrix verb phrase. In this category, the trace x_i is Ā-bound by y. The definition of governing category (21) is formulated in terms of minimal maximal projection, not in terms of minimal $\bar{S}$ or NP. This is why in (17d) the matrix VP—and not the matrix clause $\bar{S}$—is to be taken as the governing category for the nondirect object y. Confirmation for this fact is provided by the coreference possibility between the nondirect object and the matrix subject. Consider the following sentence, which was pointed out in a different context by R. S. Kayne (irrelevant details omitted):

(22)
Jean [$_{VP}$ me les$_j$ lui$_i$ fera   [acheter x_j $\bar{V}$ x_i]]
Jean   me them to him will make buy
'Jean will have me buy them to him'

In (22) the minimal maximal projection containing the governor of the nondirect object trace x_i is the matrix VP. In this VP, x_i is bound by *lui*. Since the matrix VP is the governing category for x_i or, for that matter, for the chain (*lui, x_i*), nothing prevents *Jean* and this chain from being understood as coreferential: this pronominal chain (*lui, x_i*) will still be free in its governing category. If, however, the matrix clause were considered as the governing category for the trace x_i (or for the chain (*lui, x_i*)) instead of the matrix VP, we would incorrectly predict that *Jean* and (*lui, x_i*) could not be coreferential. The reason is that the pronominal chain (*lui, x_i*) will be bound in its governing category, thus violating binding principle (B).

To summarize: We have considered the analysis of French causative constructions presented in SRS. In the embedded clausal complement of causatives, $\bar{V}$-Preposing may apply or not. In either case the embedded lexical subject functions as an opaque subject blocking the cliticization of any complement to the higher clause. However, when the embedded subject is itself cliticized, it becomes transparent and does not prevent complement cliticization.[2] These facts led to introducing the notion "accessible chain" and to replacing the notion "accessible SUBJECT" by "accessible chain" in the definition of governing category. As a consequence of this change, in delimiting the governing category for an element α, it is necessary to take into consideration not only the governor of α and its accessible SUBJECT but also the whole chain containing this SUBJECT. We will return to the consequences of this proposal in section 4.5.

4.3 Argument Structure

In the previous section we saw that cliticization of the subject in causative constructions extends the opaque domain defined by this subject. We will now consider constructions involving $\overline{V}$-Preposing where the opposite seems to hold: in these constructions the opaque domain defined by the subject is more limited than the opaque domain defined by the subject when $\overline{V}$-Preposing does not apply.

As illustrated earlier, the SSC applies in causative constructions regardless of the application of $\overline{V}$-Preposing. To be more precise, it is true that when $\overline{V}$-Preposing applies, the SSC still holds. However, the elements that obey the SSC when $\overline{V}$-Preposing applies are a subclass of the elements that obey it when $\overline{V}$-Preposing does not apply (see SRS). Thus, consider (23):

(23)

a. Marie a laissé [Paul lire   ces   romans dans la   cuisine]
    Marie let   Paul read these novels in   the kitchen
    'Marie let Paul read these novels in the kitchen'

b. *Marie y_i a laissé [Paul lire ces romans x_i]
         in it
    'Marie let Paul read these novels in it'

c. *Marie les$_i$ a laissé [Paul lire x_i dans la cuisine]
          them
    'Marie let Paul read them in the kitchen'

These examples illustrate the SSC when $\overline{V}$-Preposing does not apply: both the locative complement in (23b) and the direct object in (23c) have been cliticized outside the domain delimited by the subject *Paul* (i.e., outside the embedded clause), violating the SSC. However, when $\overline{V}$-Preposing applies, neither the locative nor the direct object is subject to the SSC. As illustrated in (24), the subject becomes transparent (see SRS, p. 180):

(24)

a. Marie a laissé [lire ces   romans à Paul dans la   cuisine]
   Marie let   read these novels to Paul in   the kitchen
   'Marie let Paul read these novels in the kitchen'

b. Marie y_i a laissé [lire ces romans à Paul x_i]
         in it
   'Marie let Paul read these novels in it'

c. Marie les$_i$ a laissé [lire x_i à Paul dans la cuisine]
         them
   'Marie let Paul read them in the kitchen'

In (24b–c) the subject is transparent, as illustrated by the fact that the locative and the direct object are cliticized onto the matrix verb. Thus, (24b–c) contrast minimally with (23b–c). After $\overline{V}$-Preposing applies, neither the direct object (which has been fronted) nor the circumstantial complements are subject to the SSC. The only complements that remain subject to the SSC are the complements subcategorized by the verb that are not fronted by $\overline{V}$-Preposing, namely, the subcategorized nondirect objects illustrated in (16) and (17) (the well-formed (b) sentences where the clitic is attached to the embedded verb are omitted):

(16)

a. Jean fera [comparer cette sonatine à Paul à une symphonie]

c. *Jean y_i fera [comparer cette sonatine à Paul $\overline{V}$ x_i]

(17)

a. Jean fera [mettre ce livre à Pierre sur l'étagère]

c. *Jean y_i fera [mettre ce livre à Pierre $\overline{V}$ x_i]

The relevant situations where the SSC applies are thus as follows (see SRS, p. 180):

(25)

a. $\overline{V}$-Preposing does not apply; the embedded subject is opaque in all cases (*Marie y a laissé Paul lire ces romans).

b. $\overline{V}$-Preposing applies; the subject behaves like a transparent subject with respect to the direct object moved by $\overline{V}$-Preposing (Marie les a laissé lire à Paul dans la cuisine).

c. $\overline{V}$-Preposing applies; the subject behaves like a transparent subject with respect to the circumstantial object not subcategorized by the verb (Marie y a laissé lire ces romans à Paul).

d. $\bar{\text{V}}$-Preposing applies; the subject behaves like an opaque subject with respect to the subcategorized nondirect object (*Jean y fera mettre ce livre à Pierre*).

To this summary should be added the result of the previous section:

e. The embedded subject is cliticized onto the causative verb and becomes transparent (*Jean leur y fera mettre ce livre*).

Cases (25a) and (25e) have been accounted for previously. Case (25a) illustrates a standard application of the SSC, and case (25e) motivated the extension of the notion "accessible SUBJECT" to "accessible chain."

Let us turn, then, to cases (25b–d). We have seen that when the subject of the embedded clause is cliticized onto the causative verb, the opaque domain defined by this subject extends to include the VP containing this causative verb. Cases (25b–d) seem to indicate that this opaque domain is narrowed when $\bar{\text{V}}$-Preposing applies. Consider the following configurations:

(26)

a. [NP causative [$_{S^*}$ NP VP ...]]
   subj

b. NP [$_{VP^*}$ clitic$_i$ + causative [x_i VP ...]]
   subj

c. NP causative [$\bar{\text{V}}$-preposed NP]
   subj
   (where X^* = governing category)

(26a) illustrates the standard application of the SSC: the domain of the subject is the embedded clause, or, in terms of the framework adopted in chapter 3, the subject NP in (26a) functions as an accessible SUBJECT (accessible chain) for the various complements of the embedded clause; the governing category for these complements will thus be the embedded clause. (26b) illustrates the extension of the domain of the subject: the accessible chain for the complements contained in the embedded clause is (clitic$_i$ ... x_i), and the minimal maximal projection containing this accessible chain is the matrix VP; therefore, the governing category for these complements is the matrix VP. (26c) illustrates a narrowing of the domain of the subject: this subject is opaque for the nondirect object subcategorized by the verb only (case (25d)) but not for the fronted direct object (case (25b)) or for the circumstantial object not subcategorized by the verb (case (25c)). In other words, the governing category seems to be neither the embedded clause nor the matrix VP.

For completeness, note that the structure where the subject of the embedded clause is cliticized onto the matrix verb and where $\overline{\text{V}}$-Preposing applies—namely, (26d)—

(26)
d. NP clitic$_i$ + causative [$\overline{\text{V}}$-preposed x_i]

is a special case of (25e). The analysis suggested to account for (25e)—replacing "accessible SUBJECT" by "accessible chain"—also accounts for (26d).

To account for (26c), let us make the following assumptions:

(27)
a. As a consequence of $\overline{\text{V}}$-Preposing, the preposed direct object is no longer c-commanded by the subject.
b. The preposed $\overline{\text{V}}$ governs and coindexes (cosuperscripts) the subject NP (see SRS).
c. When $\overline{\text{V}}$-Preposing applies, the subject NP becomes the most prominent element (= SUBJECT) with respect to the elements bearing the same index (i.e., with respect to the elements in the same argument structure).

(27b) is an instantiation of the proposal discussed in section 4.1 according to which, when $\overline{\text{V}}$-Preposing occurs in causative constructions, the subject becomes a dependent of (governed by) $\overline{\text{V}}$ and as such receives its Case-feature from the verb. (27b–c) are to be considered in light of the framework outlined in SRS section 4: it is possible to consider that a verb assigns an index to the elements it subcategorizes. This relational index is the means by which a verb marks its complements. Thus, consider the following representation (irrelevant details omitted):

(28)

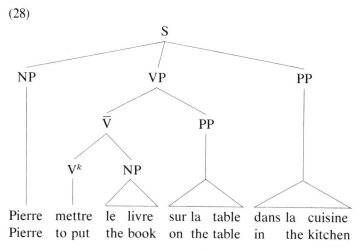

Pierre   mettre   le livre   sur la table   dans la cuisine
Pierre   to put   the book   on the table   in   the kitchen

In (28) the verb V subcategorizes for an NP and a nondirect object; it therefore assigns an index k to these elements. We will assume that the index k of V percolates up to the various projections of V ($\overline{V}$, VP) and will say that the elements bearing the same index (k in (29)) belong to the same argument structure:

(29)

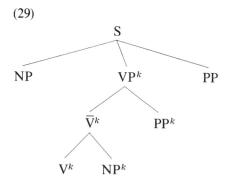

Neither the subject nor the PP immediately dominated by S is subcategorized (governed) by the verb. Consequently, they will not receive the index k of V. As we have seen, when $\overline{V}$-Preposing applies in causative constructions, the subject becomes a dependent of (governed by) $\overline{V}$ and assumes the first available grammatical function in the VP; (27b) is but the mechanism expressing this dependency. Schematically, (27b) turns (30a) into (30b) (irrelevant details omitted):

(30)

a.

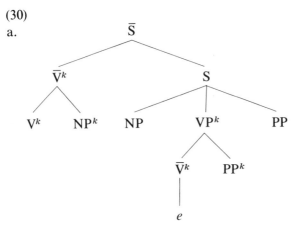

(where $[_{\bar{V}}\ e]$ is the trace left by $\bar{V}$-Preposing)

b.

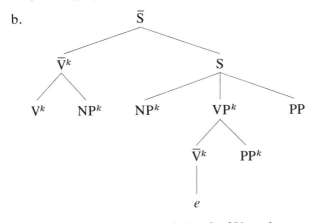

All the elements bearing the index k of V are interpreted as dependents of V; they are in the same argument structure. Thus, in (30b) the object NP, the subject NP, and the nondirect object PP are dependents of V; the subject NP is integrated into the verbal complex. In other words, (30a–b) require a special indexing rule that assigns the index of $\bar{V}$ to the subject adjacent to $\bar{V}$. Note that in (30b) the PP immediately dominated by S does not become a dependent of $\bar{V}$. This may follow from the fact that the special indexing rule that assigns the index of $\bar{V}$ to an element α requires adjacency between $\bar{V}$ and α. We must also assume that there is no rule assigning the index of VP to the PP immediately dominated by S; see Williams 1974, Hornstein 1977, Hornstein and Weinberg 1981, Huang 1982 for relevant discussion concerning PPs immediately dominated by S. These PPs enter into some selectional restrictions with the tense of the verb (Hornstein 1977) and may be viewed as being selected by INFL.

Finally, consider (27a). We have seen that as a result of $\bar{\text{V}}$-Preposing, the preposed direct object in representations (30a–b) is no longer c-commanded by the subject. Various assumptions may lead to this result. For instance, it is possible to assume either that the preposed $\bar{\text{V}}$ is Chomsky-adjoined to $\bar{\text{S}}$ or that it is adjoined, outside the clause in which it originates, to the VP containing the causative verb (see Burzio 1981 for discussion of the "landing site" of a preposed $\bar{\text{V}}$).

Returning to (30b): according to (27c), the subject NP becomes the most prominent element—the SUBJECT—with respect to the elements bearing the same index. In other words, it becomes the most prominent element with respect to the complements of the verb only. As such, the subject behaves like a transparent subject with respect to the PP immediately dominated by S. This accounts for (25c) (see (31) below). As for the complements of V—the direct and nondirect objects—the subject functions as a SUBJECT with respect to the nondirect object PP only, because it fails to c-command the direct object as assumed in (27a). Thus, for the nondirect object, the governing category containing the first accessible SUBJECT will be the minimal clause $\bar{\text{S}}$ containing this SUBJECT (the embedded clause in (31)). The nondirect object will have to cliticize in this governing category; otherwise, the empty element left by cliticization will be free in its governing category. This accounts for case (25d). For the direct object, however, this clause will not count as the governing category, since the SUBJECT of the embedded clause does not c-command this object. The minimal maximal projection containing an accessible SUBJECT for the direct object (NP in (31)) will be the higher clause in which the causative verb occurs (the matrix clause in (31)); this clause will therefore count as the governing category for the direct object. Thus, the direct object can cliticize onto the causative verb of this higher clause. This accounts for case (25b).

(31)

[$_{\bar{\text{S}}}$ NP causative [$_{\bar{\text{S}}}$ V^k NP^k_1 NP^k PP^k PP]]

The embedded $\bar{\text{S}}$ is the governing category for the subcategorized PP^k.

The matrix $\bar{\text{S}}$ is the governing category for the direct object NP^k_1.

The matrix $\bar{\text{S}}$ is the governing category for the PP immediately dominated by S.

To recapitulate, when $\bar{\text{V}}$-Preposing does not apply in a causative construction, the embedded lexical subject is an accessible SUBJECT for all the complements, whether immediately dominated by S or not. When $\bar{\text{V}}$-Preposing applies, this lexical subject may count as a SUBJECT for the elements bearing the same superscript (i.e., for the elements in the same argument structure) but not for the nonsubcategorized PPs. For the elements in the same argument structure, we must distinguish between the direct object and the subcategorized nondirect objects. For the former, the lexical subject does not count as a SUBJECT (case (25b)); for the latter, it does (case (25d)).

This analysis has certain consequences. Recall that when the subject of the embedded clause has been cliticized in a causative construction like (22), the governing category for the nondirect object is the matrix VP. Thus, the subject of the matrix clause (*Jean*) and the nondirect object of the embedded clause (*lui*, x_i) can be coreferential (irrelevant details omitted):

(22)
Jean [$_{\text{VP}}$ me les lui$_i$ fera acheter x_i]

We have said that when $\bar{\text{V}}$-Preposing applies, the governing category for the direct object of the embedded clause is the matrix clause, since it is the minimal maximal projection containing a SUBJECT for this direct object. If this analysis is correct, we expect that the pronominal direct object, unlike the pronominal nondirect object, will always be disjoint from the matrix subject; if they were coreferential, the pronominal direct object would be bound in its governing category, thus violating binding principle (B). This seems to be the case. In (32a) and (32b) the pronominal direct object (*le*) cannot be construed as coreferential with the matrix subject (*Jean*) (irrelevant details omitted):

(32)
a. Jean le　fera　　voir à　Marie
　 Jean him will let see to Marie
　 'Jean will let Marie see him'

b. Jean le　leur　　fera　　voir
　 Jean him to them will let see
　 'Jean will let them see him'

It is a striking confirmation of the proposed analysis that it provides an explanatory account for cliticization and pronominal coreference in causative constructions by appealing to the binding theory (more specifically, to principles (A) and (B)). It thus may be viewed as a confirmation of the empirical adequacy of these principles.

A final remark is in order. We have seen that at least for causatives, in delimiting the SUBJECT we must take into consideration not only the element designated as SUBJECT (AGR or [NP,S]) but also the argument structure in which this element appears. Note that the co-superscripting mechanism at work in the VP may be extended in obvious ways to a sentential level if it is assumed that INFL selects the subject NP, the predicate VP (as suggested in LGB (p. 140, fn. 20)), and the PP immediately dominated by S (since this element enters into some selectional restrictions with INFL; see Hornstein 1977):

(33)

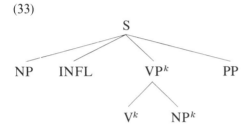

Assuming that INFL indexes the elements it selects, the subject NP, the trace VP, and the PP immediately dominated by S will be coindexed:

(34)

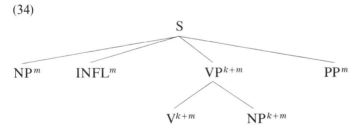

(The index assigned to VP percolates down to the head V and the complements selected by the head.)

If a representation such as (34) is adopted, (27c) may be generalized as follows:

(35)
The SUBJECT is the most prominent element with respect to the elements bearing the same index (i.e., with respect to the elements in the same argument structure).

In (33) and (34), then, AGR contained in INFL and bearing the same superscript as INFL will count as the SUBJECT for all the elements in S if the clause is finite. If the clause is nonfinite, NP will count as the SUBJECT. Note that if AGR is cosuperscripted with all the elements in S, it is plausible to assume that the specific indexing mechanism holding between AGR and the subject NP is subscripting. In a sense, this was implicit in chapter 2, where it was indicated that AGR (in some constructions) may act as an $\overline{\text{A}}$-binder of the subject.

Other questions will have to be answered before a representation such as (33)–(34) is adopted. In particular, consider the following sentence discussed in chapter 2:

(36)
we thought that pictures of each other would be on sale

As indicated in section 2.3.2, the embedded clause does not contain an accessible SUBJECT for the anaphor *each other;* the matrix clause does, however, and thus counts as the governing category for the anaphor. Given that AGR of the matrix clause counts as accessible SUBJECT for the anaphor, it must be in the same argument structure with this anaphor. This indicates that the embedded sentence and all the elements contained in it receive (by percolation) the same index as that of the matrix INFL (irrelevant details such as the indices of the VP are omitted):

(37)

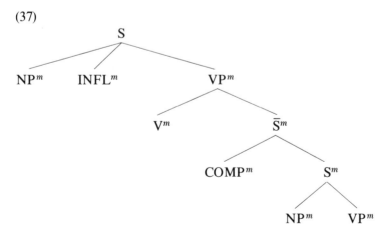

4.4 The Relevance of the Binding Theory in Causatives

The analysis just proposed to account for the distribution of clitics in causative constructions makes crucial reference to the binding theory, or for that matter to the SSC. For French causative constructions an analysis based on the binding theory is attractive because it captures a significant generalization: it provides a unified account for cliticization and pronominal coreference in these constructions. In this section we will discuss some apparent counterexamples to the relevance of the SSC or the binding theory in French causatives.

In causative constructions the subject of the embedded clause is opaque with respect to the nondirect object that has not been fronted by $\overline{\text{V}}$-Preposing, but this subject becomes transparent when cliticized onto the causative verb. The relevant contrast shows up in (38a–b) (= (17c–d)):

(38)
a. *Jean y_i fera mettre ce livre à Pierre x_i
   'Jean will have Pierre put that book on it'
b. Jean leur y_i fera mettre ce livre x_i
   'Jean will have them put that book on it'

In (38b) the subject is transparent; in (38a) it is opaque and prevents the cliticization of the nondirect complement. If this analysis is correct, we expect the subject to become transparent in constructions parallel to (38a–b) where $\overline{\text{V}}$-Preposing has not applied:

(39)
a. *Pierre y_i a laissé Paul mettre le livre x_i
   'Pierre let Paul put the book on it'
b. Pierre les y_i a laissé mettre le livre x_i
   'Pierre let them put the book on it'

As expected, in (39a) the noncliticized subject of the embedded clause is opaque and prevents the nondirect object from being cliticized onto the causative verb. In (39b), however, where the subject is cliticized onto the matrix verb, we expect this subject to become transparent and to allow the cliticization of the nondirect object onto the causative verb. The fact is that (39b) is grammatical for some speakers and ungrammatical for others. To account for this dialectal variation, some remarks are in order.

N. Chomsky (1982) suggests that cliticization is restricted to constructions in which the source of the clitic (the empty position the clitic is related to) is a θ-argument of V. Chomsky's suggestion is motivated by the facts of *ne*-cliticization from postverbal subject position in Italian. An element originating in the postverbal subject cannot cliticize onto the verb in Italian despite the fact that in Chomsky's analysis it is c-commanded by this verb (see section 2.8.1):

(40)
*... [$_{VP}$[$_{VP}$ ne   telefonato] molti]
      of-them telephone   many

In GB theory it is assumed that the subject receives its θ-role compositionally from the VP and not from the V. Since the postverbal subject is not a θ-argument of the verb, the ungrammaticality of (40) is straightforwardly accounted for.

Chomsky's suggestion is presumably too strong. For instance, it predicts that in the following sentences, in which the subject of the embedded clause is Case-governed by the matrix verb, cliticization of this subject or of an element inside this subject cannot occur, because the subject does not receive its θ-role from the matrix verb. However, the sentences are grammatical:

(41)
a. Pierre a laissé Marie partir
   'Pierre let Marie leave'
b. Pierre l'a laissé partir
   'Pierre let her leave'

Furthermore, Chomsky's analysis virtually excludes the cliticization of a nonreferential subject onto INFL (or V), since this nonreferential subject is not a θ-argument of INFL (or V) (unless it is assumed that subject cliticization is a PF phenomenon and that Chomsky's generalization holds for syntactic cliticization):

(42)
il est difficile de partir (= (66) of chapter 3)
'it is difficult to leave'

I would like to suggest that in order for an element α to be cliticized onto β, α must be a dependent of β (cf. secton 2.8.2). For the core cases, α is a dependent of β, if α is governed by β. This proposal has a number of consequences. It excludes the syntactic cliticization of a subject onto a verb since the subject is not governed by V. It is possible to consider that the subject cliticizes onto INFL. To the extent that the syntactic cliticization of the subject takes place at all, this is a desirable result, since we assumed that the relation between a clitic and its trace is an anaphoric relation subject to the binding theory. If the subject were to cliticize onto the V (or VP), the clitic would not be able to c-command its trace; thus, the trace would be left free. In case it proves necessary to assume that the cliticized subject ends up on the verb in the surface structure, a readjustment rule such as the one that attaches INFL onto a verb will give the desired result. The same considerations could be extended to PPs immediately dominated by S such as the locative in (43):[3]

(43)
Jean y a vu Pierre
'Jean saw Pierre in it'

For an element α to cliticize onto β, then, two conditions must be met:

(44)
a. No binding theory violation occurs.
b. α is a dependent of β.

In SRS Rouveret and Vergnaud suggest that in French causative constructions the embedded predicate becomes "thematically related" to the causative verb. Informally speaking, the causative and the embedded predicate form a complex predicate. In that case, the arguments of the embedded predicate become arguments of the complex predicate. Furthermore, Rouveret and Vergnaud indicate that this complex predicate formation occurs only when $\overline{\text{V}}$-Preposing applies.

With this in mind, let us return to (39a–b) where $\overline{\text{V}}$-Preposing did not apply. Given the foregoing discussion, it is not surprising that some speakers do not accept (39b) as a grammatical sentence. Assuming with Rouveret and Vergnaud that this complex predicate formation occurs only when $\overline{\text{V}}$-Preposing applies, condition (44b) will not be satisfied; thus, y will not cliticize onto the causative verb. For the speakers who accept (39b), it may be that complex predicate formation always occurs in causative constructions even when $\overline{\text{V}}$-Preposing does not apply.

Now consider a representation where $\overline{\text{V}}$-Preposing applies—namely, (38b), repeated as (45) (irrelevant details omitted):

(45)

Jean leur$_j$ y$_i$ fera mettre ce livre x_j [$_\bar{v}$[$_\bar{v}$ V NP x_i]]

'Jean will have them put the book on it'

(where V is the trace of *mettre* and NP that of *ce livre*)

In (45) the chain containing *leur* is the relevant accessible chain for the trace of the clitic. The minimal maximal projection containing this accessible chain is the matrix VP. The verb that satisfies (44b) is the complex predicate *fera mettre*. Strictly speaking, the trace of the clitic *y* is not directly governed by *fera mettre* in (45). It is governed instead by the trace of the preposed *mettre*, which forms a complex predicate with *fera:* there is a government relation between *fera mettre* and the trace of *y* via the trace of the preposed verb. A somewhat parallel case of indirect government in Spanish is discussed in Torrego 1984.

Finally, consider the following sentences discussed in SRS:

(46)

a. *Marie y   a fait se   rencontrer Pierre et   Jean
   Marie in it had   each other meet   Pierre and Jean
   'Marie had Pierre and Jean meet there'

b. *Marie les   y   a fait se   rencontrer
   Marie them in it had   each other meet
   'Marie had them meet there'

One way of accounting for the ungrammaticality of (46b) is to assume that complex predicate formation does not apply there—that is, that condition (44b) is not satisfied. In that case the clitic *y* cannot attach to the causative verb *faire*. What prevents complex predicate formation from applying in (46b)?

Essentially, when complex predicate formation occurs, the embedded verb loses the ability to assign Case and/or θ-role; that is, it is no longer an autonomous element. Instead, it is the complex predicate that assigns Case and/or θ-role. Let us assume, as argued in Aoun 1981b, that clitics absorb the Case and/or the θ-role assigned by the element they are attached to. If this is correct, the fact that a clitic is attached to the embedded verb clearly indicates that complex predicate formation did not apply: this verb is still an autonomous Case- and/or θ-role-assigner, assigning the Case and/or θ-role that will be absorbed by the clitic. (For relevant considerations along similar lines, see Wehrli 1983.)

Another apparent counterexample to the relevance of the binding theory (or the SSC) in French causative constructions involves sentences such as the following pair from Wehrli 1983:

(47)
a. Jean fait douter Marie de ses capacités
   'Jean makes Marie doubt her abilities'
b. Jean en fait douter Marie
   'Jean makes Marie doubt them'

Since the complement of the embedded clause in (47a) has not been fronted by $\bar{V}$-Preposing, we expect it to be subject to the SSC. In other words, we expect the cliticization of this complement onto the causative verb to yield an ungrammatical result. This is not the case, however, as indicated by the grammaticality of (47b). In brief, the SSC seems to make a wrong prediction.

The problem raised by sentences (47a–b) dissolves if the following remarks are taken into consideration. As indicated in LGB (section 2.5) and in Stowell 1981, Case assignment requires adjacency: for a direct object to receive accusative Case, it must be adjacent to its Case-assigner, namely, the verb. (See Stowell 1981 and Van Riemsdijk 1981 for extensive discussion of the adjacency requirement and its status in French.) In (47a) the subject, which becomes a dependent of the fronted verb, receives accusative Case from this verb by virtue of being governed by and adjacent to it. In (47b), where cliticization takes place, nothing prevents us from considering that the empty element coindexed with the clitic has been fronted with the verb by $\bar{V}$-Preposing. In that case the representation of (47b) would be (48):

(48)
Jean en$_i$ fait [$_{\bar{V}}$ douter x_i] Marie

Thus, the empty element x escapes the effect of the SSC, because it is fronted with the embedded verb by $\bar{V}$-Preposing. The adjacency requirement is not violated in (48) since the non-Case-marked empty element x, like other non-Case-marked empty elements, does not count for adjacency (on this matter, see LGB (p. 94) and Pulleyblank 1980).

Finally, a third type of problem facing an SSC account for the distribution of clitics in French causative constructions is illustrated by the following sentence:

(49)
Jean lui fait   porter une lettre à Marie
Jean him makes bring a   letter to Marie
'Jean makes him bring a letter to Marie'

Examples such as this are discussed in Ruwet 1972 and Kayne 1975. Here, the clitic *lui* is interpreted as the subject of the embedded clause and not as the indirect object of the verb *porter*. As indicated in Wehrli 1983, in order for the SSC to account for (49) it is necessary to assume that $\overline{\text{V}}$-Preposing fronts the verb and the direct object but not the indirect object. Not being fronted, the indirect object will be subject to the SSC (section 4.3). In brief, the structure of (49) is (50a) and not (50b):

(50)
a. Jean fait [$_{\overline{\text{V}}}$ porter une lettre] à NP à NP
                                                subj IO
b. Jean fait [porter une lettre à NP] à NP
                                    IO   subj

However, such an analysis directly conflicts with Ruwet's observation that for the speakers accepting (51) it is the second *à*-phrase and not the first that is understood as the subject of the infinitival verb:

(51)
Jean fait porter une lettre à Marie à Paul
'Jean makes Paul bring a letter to Marie'

Wehrli indicates that the correct interpretation of (51) follows if the whole phrase has been raised by $\overline{\text{V}}$-Preposing; that is, it follows if the representation of (49) is (50b). But if so, the cliticization of the indirect object in (49) should escape the effect of the SSC: in other words, there should be an interpretation where *lui* is construed as the indirect object of the verb *porter*.

For the argument to go through, it must be assumed that the ordering of the *à*-phrases in (51) is not a superficial phenomenon. The following considerations suggest that this is the case. Following Williams 1980, let us distinguish between "external"and "internal" arguments. Roughly speaking, the subject (on a sentential level) is the external argument and the complements are the internal arguments. Now recall from section 2.2.1 that the characterization of the subject in an NP seems to be determined according to the thematic hierarchy (52), illustrated in (53):

(52)
a. Possessor (or source)
b. Agent
c. Theme

(53)
a. le portrait d'Aristote de Rembrandt de Pierre
   'the portrait of Aristotle of Rembrandt of   Pierre'
        (theme)   (agent)   (possessor)
b. le portrait d'Aristote de Rembrandt
   'the portrait of Aristotle of Rembrandt'
        (theme)   (agent)
c. le portrait d'Aristote
   'the portrait of Aristotle'
        (theme)

According to (52), *de Pierre* will be characterized as the subject in (53a), *de Rembrandt* as the subject in (53b), and *d'Aristote* as the subject in (53c). Recall also that this hierarchy holds for *de NP* arguments only. By assuming that *de NP* complements are real NPs and not PPs (i.e., that *de* is simply a Case-marker, as argued in Vergnaud 1974), we can say that the thematic hierarchy inside an NP holds for NP arguments but not for PPs: only an NP can be subject. But notice also that the subject in (53) is always the most peripheral with respect to the other arguments: it is the "external" argument with respect to thé other arguments. In brief, there seems to be a strategy that places the subject at the periphery of the NP in (53).

It is plausible to suggest that a similar strategy is at work in (51): in the sequence of two *à NP*'s, the subject is the more peripheral. In causative constructions this strategy seems to hold for *à NP*'s in case of ambiguity. If for some reason (for instance, selectional restrictions) no ambiguity arises, then the subject does not need to be the more peripheral. This is shown by the two possible orderings in (54):

(54)
a. Jean fera comparer cette sonatine à Paul à une symphonie
b. Jean fera comparer cette sonatine à une symphonie à Paul
   'Jean will have Paul compare that sonata with a symphony'

Moreover, the strength of this strategy seems to vary from speaker to speaker. For these reasons, it is plausible to view this phenomenon as a disambiguating strategy rather than an absolute syntactic constraint. If this approach is correct, the problem raised with respect to (49) dissolves: the representation of (49) will be as in (50a) even though the subject is the more peripheral in (51). In other words, sentences such as (49) do not constitute a problem for an SSC account for the distribution of clitics in French causative constructions.

The analysis proposed in this section is certainly not exhaustive. Obviously, there are many other aspects of cliticization in causative constructions, such as the various cooccurrence restrictions between clitics, that I have not discussed. My main concern has been to study the behavior of the SSC, or for that matter the binding theory, in French causative constructions. This behavior appears to be of some theoretical interest: it has motivated replacing the notion of "accessible SUBJECT" by "accessible chain" and has indicated that in determining what counts as SUBJECT, the notion "argument structure" is relevant; that is, the SUBJECT is the most prominent element with respect to the other elements in the same argument structure.

4.5 Thematic Chains

As a result of replacing "accessible SUBJECT" with "accessible chain," it is necessary in delimiting the governing category for an element α to take into consideration not only the governor of α and its accessible SUBJECT but also the whole chain containing this SUBJECT:

(55)
β is a *governing category* for α iff β is the minimal maximal projection containing α, a governor of α, and a chain accessible to α.
$(= (21))$

(56)
A chain α is *accessible* to β iff α contains a SUBJECT accessible to β. $(= (19))$

Let us consider the consequences of this proposal. The following sentences appear prima facie to pose some problems for extending the notion "accessible SUBJECT" to "accessible chain":

(57)
a. *who$_i$ did they$_j$ expect [t_i [x_i AGR would see each other$_j$]]
b. *who$_i$ did they$_j$ believe [x_i to have seen each other$_j$]
c. *he$_i$ seems to the men$_j$ [t_i to like each other$_j$]

d. *John$_i$ $\begin{Bmatrix} \text{strikes} \\ \text{impresses} \end{Bmatrix}$ us$_j$ [t_i as like each other$_j$]

In (57a–b) the accessible SUBJECT for the reciprocal (*each other*) is AGR, and the governor is *see*. If AGR forms a chain with the subject x and its antecedent (the *wh*-element), (57a) will constitute a problem for the notion of accessible chain. The putative chain will be (*who, t, x, AGR*), and the governing category of *each other* will thus be the matrix clause; it is the minimal category containing the whole accessible chain and the governor of the reciprocal, *see*. The sentence will incorrectly be marked as grammatical, since the reciprocal is A-bound by *they* in this governing category. However, no problem arises if AGR does not form a chain with the subject x or if the variable in subject position does not form a chain with the *wh*-element in COMP (e.g., if chains are restricted to A-chains; see section 2.10). Under the first option the accessible chain will be AGR; under the second it will be (x, AGR).[4] Under both options the embedded clause will be the governing category for the reciprocal, since it is the minimal category containing the chain accessible to this reciprocal: (57a) will correctly be excluded by the binding theory, since the reciprocal is free in its governing category.

The same reasoning leads to the conclusion that in (57b) the variable in subject position does not form a chain with the *wh*-element in COMP. Suppose the *wh*-element and the variable in subject position form a unique chain; since the variable is an accessible SUBJECT for the reciprocal, the minimal category containing the accessible chain will be the matrix clause. The sentence will incorrectly be marked as grammatical since the reciprocal is A-bound by *they* in this governing category. However, if the variable in subject position does not form a chain with the *wh*-element in COMP, no problem arises. The accessible chain will be (x), and the embedded clause will be the governing category, since it is the minimal category containing the accessible chain.[5] The reciprocal is A-free in this governing category, and the sentence will correctly be excluded by the binding theory. We therefore conclude that, for the notion of accessible chain, the variable and its antecedent in COMP do not form a chain.

In (57c) the trace t and the raised subject *he* are undoubtedly in a single chain, which is accessible to *each other:* the governing category containing this accessible chain and the governor of *each other* (*like*) is the matrix clause. The sentence should be well formed, since the reciprocal is not free in its governing category. It might be suggested that the sentence is not grammatical because the potential A-binder of the reciprocal (*the men*) fails to c-command it. However, this proposal will face some problems. Consider the following sentences noted by N. Chomsky:

(58)
a. I spoke angrily to the men about each other
b. *I spoke angrily about the men to each other

Case (58b) is accounted for by the binding theory, since *each other* is not c-commanded by *the men*. Case (58a) indicates that the c-command requirement is satisfied. It is therefore possible to consider the phrase *to the men* as an NP along the lines discussed in Vergnaud 1974, George 1980, and Jaeggli 1982 with *to* a Case-marker. (58a) will be grammatical with binding of *each other* by *to the men*. It thus appears that the c-command account of the ungrammaticality of (57c) cannot be maintained. Note that the phrase *to the men* in (57c) cannot easily be questioned:

(59)
???to which men$_j$ does he$_i$ seem x_j [t_i to like each other$_i$]

This sentence is to be contrasted with (60b):

(60)
a. it seems to the men that he likes Bill
b. to which men$_j$ does it seem x_j that he likes Bill

A. Rouveret has pointed out to me that a similar contrast holds in French. A parallel contrast exists between (61a) and (61b), where $\overline{\text{S}}$-Deletion does not occur:

(61)
a. *which man$_j$ did he$_i$ seem to x_j [t_i to like Bill]
b. ?which man$_j$ did he appeal to x_j [PRO to like Bill]

The contrast between (59) and (60b) or the one between (61a) and (61b) may be accounted for along the following lines. It is indicated in LGB that proper government requires some kind of adjacency. We will assume that $\overline{\text{S}}$-Deletion requires adjacency, and moreover that an A-position, but not a peripheral position ($\overline{\text{A}}$-position), breaks the adjacency requirement necessary for the $\overline{\text{S}}$-to-S rule to apply between the matrix verb and the embedded clause.[6] With this in mind, consider again (57c):

(57)

c. he$_i$ seems to the men$_j$ [t$_i$ to like each other$_j$]

The verb *seems* and the embedded clause are separated by the phrase *to the men*. Assuming that this phrase is an A-position, $\overline{\text{S}}$-Deletion will not apply. Under the assumption that $\overline{\text{S}}$ breaks a chain, *he* and the trace *t* will be in separate chains. The sentence will be ruled out by the θ-Criterion, since neither the chain containing *he* nor the one containing the trace will receive a θ-role: the first because it is not a θ-position, the second because it lacks Case. Assuming, however, that the phrase *to the men* is in a peripheral position ($\overline{\text{A}}$-position) with respect to the verb *seem,* the phrase *to the men* will not break the adjacency requirement necessary for the $\overline{\text{S}}$-to-S rule to apply: *he* and its trace *t* in (57c) will be in the same chain. This chain will be assigned a θ-role, and the sentence will be grammatical. However, in a sentence like (60a) where no $\overline{\text{S}}$-Deletion need occur,

(60)

a. it seems to the men that he likes Bill

the phrasal element intervening between the matrix verb and the embedded clause may be in an A-position or in a peripheral position ($\overline{\text{A}}$-position) with respect to the matrix verb.

In brief, the phrasal position occurring after *seem* may be ambiguously characterized as an A-position or as an $\overline{\text{A}}$-position as in (60a). However, in a context where $\overline{\text{S}}$-Deletion must occur, the representation where this phrasal position is treated as an A-position will prevent the application of the rule, and it will be excluded by the θ-Criterion. The only remaining possibility, then, is to treat the phrasal position as an $\overline{\text{A}}$-position in a context where $\overline{\text{S}}$-Deletion must occur.[7]

(62)

a. NP seem to NP [$_S$ *t* VP $_{\text{infinitival clause}}$]
    (*to NP* is in an $\overline{\text{A}}$-position where $\overline{\text{S}}$-Deletion must occur (see (57c))
b. NP seem to NP [$_{\overline{\text{S}}}$ NP VP]
    (*to NP* may be in an A-position or an $\overline{\text{A}}$-position (see (60a))

In Aoun 1981b I suggest that an element in an $\overline{\text{A}}$-position cannot be extracted by movement rules, and I propose a relativized definition of A- and $\overline{\text{A}}$-position. If this suggestion is correct, the present analysis predicts that since the position in which *to the men* occurs in (57c) is necessarily an $\overline{\text{A}}$-position, no movement will take place from this position. In (60a), however, the position of *to the men* may ambiguously be characterized as an A-position or an $\bar{\text{A}}$-position. Thus, there is a representation in which *to the men* may be extracted by a movement rule. Both predictions are fulfilled. Since the position *to the men* in (57c) is an $\bar{\text{A}}$-position, that sentence will be ruled out by the binding theory: the reciprocal is A-free in its governing category. As illustrated in (59), (60b), and (61a), when $\bar{\text{S}}$-Deletion does not occur, *to the men* can be questioned, and when $\bar{\text{S}}$-Deletion does occur, it cannot.

Finally, consider (57d), which is repeated here:

(57)

d. *John_i $\begin{Bmatrix} \text{strikes} \\ \text{impresses} \end{Bmatrix}$ us_j [$_\text{S}$ t_i as like each other$_j$]

Here, the NP *John* has been raised from the subject position of the small clause (S) (an analysis of small clauses may be found in LGB, section 2.6). The ungrammaticality of this sentence constitutes a problem for the proposal that the notion "accessible SUBJECT" is to be replaced by the notion "accessible chain." The putative chain will be (*John, t*). The governing category for *each other* will thus be the matrix clause: it is the minimal category containing the whole accessible chain and the governor (*strikes* or *impresses*) of the reciprocal. The sentence will incorrectly be marked as grammatical, since the reciprocal is A-bound by *us* in the governing category. Note that the account suggested for (57c) does not carry over: in (57d) *us* is in an A-position, as indicated by the fact that it can be extracted:

(63)

who_i did John $\begin{Bmatrix} \text{strike} \\ \text{impress} \end{Bmatrix}$ x_i as being intelligent

However, recall from section 3.7 the discussion of "parasitic gaps"— namely, constructions where two empty elements are related to a single operator:

(64)

a. which articles did John file e_1 without reading e_2
b. this is the kind of food you must cook e_1 before you eat e_2

Following Chomsky 1982, we referred to e_1 as the *licensing variable* and to e_2 as the *parasitic gap*. In parasitic gap constructions the licensing variable cannot c-command the parasitic gap. If it does, the derivation will be excluded by the binding theory, since the parasitic gap, which is a variable, will be A-bound by the licensing variable e_1. In other words, parasitic gaps may provide insight into the constituent structure of a sentence: in sentences involving parasitic gaps, the position filled by the licensing variable does not c-command the position filled by the parasitic gap.

With this in mind, consider the following sentences, which have the same status as other parasitic gap constructions such as (64a–b); the judgments are those of N. Chomsky and other speakers consulted:

(65)

a. who did the pamphlets strike e_1 [$_S$ as being insulting to e_2]

b. who did John impress e_1 [$_S$ as being concerned about e_2]

Sentences (65a–b) are parallel to (57d): they all involve a small clause. Since parasitic gaps are allowed, we conclude that in (65a–b) the position occupied by the licensing variable e_1 does not c-command the parasitic gap e_2. Since (57d) has the same representation as (65a–b), the position filled by *us* does not c-command the position filled by the reciprocal *each other*. Therefore, *us* cannot A-bind *each other*. (57d) will be excluded by the binding theory: the reciprocal is free in its governing category. In short, (57d) does not constitute a problem if the notion "accessible SUBJECT" is replaced by the notion "accessible chain."

To summarize: We have considered sentences that may be problematic for the idea of extending the notion "accessible SUBJECT" to "accessible chain," finding that at least for the notion "accessible chain," these problems may be overcome if the empty element in subject position does not form a chain with its antecedent—the *wh*-element—in COMP (see (57a–b)). Moreover, in raising constructions the "object" of the verb that triggers $\bar{S}$-Deletion is in an $\bar{A}$-position with respect to this verb and thus cannot bind an A-anaphor (see (57c)). Finally, in constructions involving small clauses the object of the verb does not c-command the small clause and thus cannot bind an anaphor in this clause (see (57d)).

Let us now characterize the notion "chain" relevant to the definition of accessible chain. We have seen that the clitic that occupies an $\bar{A}$-position and the empty element in subject position coindexed with this clitic may constitute an accessible chain, as in (66a). Similarly, the trace of an NP and its antecedent may constitute an accessible chain, as in (66b). However, a *wh*-trace and its antecedent may not constitute a chain, as shown in (66c):

(66)

a. clitic$_i$... x_i...   — constitute a chain
b. NP$_i$... t_i...   — constitute a chain
c. wh_i... t_i...   — do not constitute a chain

If we restrict the notion "chain" to "A-chain" (i.e., to chains whose members are in A-positions, as in section 2.10), we automatically exclude (66c), since the wh-element in COMP is in an $\overline{\text{A}}$-position, but we also exclude (66a) under the assumption that clitics are in an $\overline{\text{A}}$-position (see section 2.6.1). If we do not make this restriction, however, we will need to exclude (66c) from the relevant set of chains. This may be taken as indicating that clitics are in A-positions, contrary to the evidence presented in section 2.6.1. Another possibility may be to assume that the relevant notion is that of θ-*chain*—a chain whose members are in positions that may (but need not) receive a θ-role. This proposal will include chains whose members are in A-positions (an A-position may receive a θ-role) or clitic positions, if it is assumed as suggested in section 3.6.2 that clitics, although in $\overline{\text{A}}$-positions, may receive a θ-role from the elements they are attached to or inherit a θ-role from the NP position they are coindexed with. It will also correctly prevent wh-elements in COMP from being in a chain since the COMP-position neither receives nor inherits a θ-role.[8] If the latter proposal is adopted, the definition of chain adopted in section 2.10 will have to be reformulated in obvious ways.

4.6 Summary

We have seen that in the embedded clausal complement of causatives, $\overline{\text{V}}$-Preposing may or may not apply. In these constructions the embedded lexical subject functions as an opaque subject blocking the cliticization of any complement to the higher clause. However, when this embedded subject is itself cliticized, it becomes transparent and does not prevent such cliticization.

To account for this, we introduced the notion "accessible chain" and substituted it for "accessible SUBJECT" in the definition of governing category. As a result, in delimiting the governing category for an element α, it is necessary to take into consideraton not only the governor of α and its accessible SUBJECT but also the whole chain containing this SUBJECT. This proposal amounts to treating the trace and its antecedent(s) as a discontinuous element that is relevant as a whole for delimiting the governing category.

Pursuing the study of causative constructions, we noted (following SRS) that when $\bar{\text{V}}$-Preposing does not apply, the embedded lexical subject is an accessible SUBJECT to all complements, whether immediately dominated by S or not. However, when $\bar{\text{V}}$-Preposing does apply, this lexical subject counts as SUBJECT for the elements bearing the same superscript (i.e., for elements in the same argument structure). In other words, to identify the SUBJECT, we must consider not only the nature of the element (AGR or [NP,S]) and its position but also the argument structure in which it appears: an element may not be the most prominent (SUBJECT) with respect to other elements that are not in the same argument structure.

The analysis of causative constructions put forward in sections 4.2 and 4.3 provides a unified account for cliticization and pronominal coreference. This is exactly as expected if the domain in which an anaphor (such as clitic-trace) must be bound and the one in which a pronoun must be free are both defined in terms of SUBJECT. It also provides a means to specify the relevant notion of chain in the grammar: the notion "θ-chain" (thematic chain).

Chapter 5
Binding, Negation, and Quantification

In chapter 1 I claimed that $\bar{\text{A}}$-anaphors, like A-anaphors, may be overt or not and may bear an independent θ-role or not. Thus, they may be characterized with respect to the features [$\pm\theta$-role], [$\pm$overt]:

(1)

$\bar{\text{A}}$-anaphors

a. [$+\theta$-role, $+$overt] : reciprocals in Italian
b. [$-\theta$-role, $+$overt] :
c. [$-\theta$-role, $-$overt] : clitic-trace
d. [$+\theta$-role, $-$overt] : *wh*-trace

In chapter 1 I also argued that the two members of the Italian reciprocal expression *l'uno* . . . *l'altro* 'each other' enter into a binding relation: *l'altro* is an $\bar{\text{A}}$-anaphor bound by *l'uno*. Presumably, *l'altro*, which is in A-position, bears the θ-role assigned to the reciprocal expression.

In chapter 2, where the binding theory was generalized to a theory of A-binding and $\bar{\text{A}}$-binding, I argued that the relation holding between the *wh*-trace and the *wh*-antecedent is an $\bar{\text{A}}$-anaphoric relation: the *wh*-trace is a nonovert $\bar{\text{A}}$-anaphor that bears an independent θ-role. In chapters 3 and 4 I argued that the empty element coindexed with the clitic is an anaphor $\bar{\text{A}}$-bound by the clitic.

Despite the fact that *wh*-traces and clitic-traces are both $\bar{\text{A}}$-anaphors, they display different behavior. For instance, the former, but not the latter, escape the effect of the Specified Subject Condition (SSC). The difference between the two kinds of $\bar{\text{A}}$-anaphors traces back to the fact that a *wh*-trace is a namelike expression bearing an independent θ-role: as namelike expressions, *wh*-traces are subject to principle (C) of the binding theory; as anaphors, they are subject to principle (A). It thus follows that a *wh*-trace may escape the SSC at a sentential level.

The empty element coindexed with the clitic, however, is not a name. This is because the clitic itself is the element that requires a θ-role. Since this clitic is in the same chain with the empty element it is coindexed with, it follows from the θ-Criterion that the empty element cannot be a referential element bearing an independent θ-role. Thus, the empty element coindexed with the clitic is subject to binding principle (A) and therefore will obey the SSC.

In this chapter I will examine other instances of the generalized binding theory and of $\overline{\text{A}}$-anaphors that may be characterized in terms of (1a–d). The study of negative *ne . . . personne* constructions in Romance will reveal the existence of three distinct dialects. In the first, *personne* has the same distribution as variables; in the second, it has the same distribution as anaphors; and in the third, it has the same distribution as names. I will argue that a unified account for these dialectal variations may be provided by an approach incorporating the generalized binding theory. In the first dialect, *personne* is subject to binding principles (A) and (C); in the second, it is subject to binding principle (A); and in the third, it is subject to binding principle (C).

Quantifiers may be classified with respect to their scope properties into three types: those that are essentially clause-bound, those that are not clause-bound and display the standard subject-object asymmetry characteristic of elements subject to the ECP, and finally those that are not clause-bound and do not display any subject-object asymmetry. It will appear that this "classification" is parallel to that of the three *ne . . . personne* dialects in Romance. Quantifiers that display the asymmetry (or more precisely the empty elements left by their LF extraction) are subject to binding principles (A) and (C); those that are clause-bound are subject to binding principle (A); and those that are not clause-bound and do not display any asymmetry are subject to binding principle (C).

Finally, I will turn to the case of overt $\overline{\text{A}}$-anaphors that do not bear an overt θ-role, arguing that this case is illustrated in existential constructions by the nonreferential *there*.

5.1 The Scope of Negation

In this section I will discuss the distribution of negative expressions in Romance languages. Focusing on the quantifier *ninguno* 'no one' in Spanish, I will suggest that a puzzling array of facts may be accounted for by the *i*-within-*i* Condition, the well-formedness condition that plays a role in GB theory in characterizing the governing category in which an A-anaphor must be bound (cf. section 2.3.2).

As indicated in Jaeggli 1982, the analysis of *nessuno* 'no one' outlined for Italian in Rizzi 1982a and discussed in section 2.8.1 can be extended to Spanish to account for the behavior of negative expressions such as *ninguno*.

In Spanish, as in Italian, preverbal *ninguno* does not tolerate *no* attached to the verb, whereas postverbal *ninguno* requires it (examples from Jaeggli 1982:129):

(2)
a. no vino ninguno
    neg came no one

b. *vino ninguno
c. ninguno vino
d. *ninguno no vino
    'no one came'

(3)
a. no veo a ninguno
    neg see no one

b. *veo a ninguno
c. ?a ninguno veo
d. *a ninguno no veo
    'I don't see anyone'

This may be accounted for by a PF rule that deletes *no* if there is a preverbal *ninguno* (see Jaeggli 1982 and Rizzi 1982a for a characterization of this rule):

(4)
no → $\emptyset$ / ninguno ____ X

In LF the meaning of *ninguno* is combined with *no* to form NEG [$\exists x$], that is, *there is no x* or *it is not the case that there is an x*. The LF representation of (2a) and (2c), for instance, will be as follows:

(5)
a. NEG [$\exists x$] [vino x]
b. NEG [$\exists x$] [x vino]

Recall, moreover, that the analysis of Italian *nessuno* (Spanish *ninguno*) was based on the following assumptions originally suggested for French in Kayne 1981b:

(6)

a. The particle *ne* (*no* in Spanish) is a scope operator determining the scope of *nessuno* (*ninguno*).

b. *Nessuno* (*ninguno*) undergoes Quantifier-Movement in LF.

In light of (4) and (6), consider the following sentence:

(7)
no quiero   que venga ninguno
neg (I) want that comes no one
'I don't want anyone to come'

According to (6), (7) will have the following interpretation (irrelevant details omitted):

(8)
NEG [$\exists x$] [quiero [que venga x]]

However, (9) cannot have the same interpretation as (7):

(9)
no quiero que ninguno venga
'I don't want that no one come'

(10)
*NEG [$\exists x$] [quiero [$_S$ que x venga]]

Rather, it has the following interpretation:

(11)
NEG [quiero [$_{\bar{S}}$ que NEG [$\exists x$] x venga]]

As indicated earlier, the ungrammaticality of (10) illustrates an ECP effect: the variable x is left in non–properly governed position. In terms of the generalized binding theory, the variable x in (10) is not $\bar{A}$-bound in its governing category, the embedded $\bar{S}$, thus violating principle (A) of the binding theory. D. Salammanca and E. Torrego (personal communication) point out that there seem to be speakers for whom interpretation (10) is available. I will return to this observation in section 5.2.

Now consider the following sentences:

(12)

a. *la foto de ninguno está en la mesa
   'the picture of no one is on the table'
b. no vi la foto de ninguno
   'I have seen the picture of no one'

The ungrammaticality of the French sentence corresponding to (12a) was first pointed out in Milner 1979. In preverbal subject position, *ninguno* may not appear inside NP. In object position, however, it may. To account for the contrast between (12a) and (12b), I would like to suggest that:

(13)

a. *No* is in INFL and has the same index as AGR.
b. *Ninguno* and the particle *no* are coindexed.

(13a) amounts to assuming that INFL has an index that percolates to the elements dominated by INFL. Note that the percolation is not subject to the *i*-within-*i* Condition. This is because all the elements contained in INFL may be viewed as features (and not independent categories) specifying the same matrix INFL: thus, INFL will contain the set of features [±tense], [αnumber, βgender, γperson] (i.e., AGR), and [±negative] specifying the matrix INFL. Instead of a deletion rule such as (4), which deletes *no* when preceded by *ninguno,* the grammar will contain a rule that specifies the contexts in which [±negative] is phonetically realized. As for (13b), it may be thought of as an instantiation of the informal observation mentioned above according to which the meaning of *ninguno* is combined with that of *no* to form NEG [$\exists x$]. Given (13a–b), the contrast between (12a) and (12b) will be accounted for by the *i*-within-*i* Condition.

According to (13a–b), the representation of (12a–b) will be as follows prior to the deletion rule (4) and Quantifier-Raising:

(14)

a. *[$_{NP_p}$ la foto de ninguno] [$_{INFL}$ no$_p$ AGR$_p$] ...
b. [$_{INFL}$ no$_p$ AGR$_p$] vi [$_{NP}$ la foto de ninguno$_p$]

In (14a) the subject NP has the same index as an element (*ninguno*) contained in it; the derivation will be filtered out by the *i*-within-*i* Condition. For the speakers I have consulted, the sentence is still ungrammatical (at best slightly less ungrammatical) when the subject is in postverbal subject position:

(15)

no está en la mesa la foto de ninguno
'the picture of no one is on the table'

This analysis predicts that the NP *la foto de ninguno* should be allowed in preverbal subject position if the scope indicator *no* is in a clause different from the one containing the NP, as in (16):[1]

(16)

[$_s$ no$_p$ ... [$_s$[$_{NP_k}$ la foto de ninguno$_p$] AGR$_k$ ...]]

Here, *no* (which is in the matrix clause) is coindexed with *ninguno,* and the subject NP (like all subjects) is coindexed with the AGR of the embedded clause in which it appears. (16) does not violate the *i*-within-*i* Condition, and the derivation should therefore be grammatical. This appears to be the case, as the grammaticality of (17) attests:

(17)

no quiero que la foto de ninguno esté en la mesa
'I want the picture of no one to be on the table'

Another prediction of this analysis concerns the interpretation of (17). Recall that of the two interpretations allowed for (9), one (namely, (10)) is ruled out by the ECP (or by the generalized binding principles):

(9)

no quiero que ninguno venga
'I don't want that no one come'

(10)

*NEG [$\exists x$] [quiero [$_s$ que x venga]]

(11)

NEG [quiero [$_{\bar{s}}$ que NEG [$\exists x$] x venga]]

For (17) the proposed analysis predicts that the opposite holds. The interpretation corresponding to (10) where *ninguno* is associated with the matrix *no* is the only possible one:

(18)

NEG [$\exists x$] [quiero [$_{\bar{s}}$ que [$_{NP}$ la foto de x] esté en la mesa]]

(19)

*NEG [quiero que [NEG [$\exists x$] [$_{NP}$ la foto de x] esté en la mesa]]

Prior to Quantifier-Raising and to the application of rule (4), (19) will have the following representation (irrelevant details omitted):

(20)
*no quiero que [$_{NP_p}$ la foto de ninguno$_p$] no$_p$ AGR$_p$ esté en la mesa

Here, the subject of the embedded clause has the same index as *ninguno;* the derivation will be filtered out by the *i*-within-*i* Condition.

This prediction is fulfilled; the only possible interpretation for (17) is the one corresponding to (18). This can be clearly seen if (17) is followed by *quiero que la foto de Pedro esté en la mesa* 'I want the picture of Pedro to be on the table'; (21) is a contradiction:

(21)
no quiero que la foto de ninguno esté en la mesa; quiero que la foto de Pedro esté en la mesa
'I want the picture of no one to be on the table; I want the picture of Pedro to be on the table'

In sum, the *i*-within-*i* Condition accounts for the ungrammaticality of sentences where [$_{NP}$ Det N de ninguno] appears in subject position of the matrix clause (14a), for the grammaticality of sentences where the NP containing *ninguno* and the scope marker *no* are in different clauses (17), and for the nonavailability of some interpretations in the latter context.

5.2 Binding and Negation

Other aspects of negative constructions in Romance languages appear to be relevant to the notion of $\overline{\text{A}}$-anaphor that we are discussing.

In French, *personne* must occur in the same environment as *ne*. When *ne* and *personne* occur in the same clause, no restriction exists; *personne* can appear in any position (subject, object, etc.) except the one illustrated in (23):

(22)
a. Jean ne voit personne
   Jean neg sees body
   'Jean sees nobody'
b. personne ne voit Jean
   body   neg sees Jean
   'nobody sees Jean'

(23)
*la   photo   de personne   n'est   sur la   table
the picture of   body   neg is on   the table

The ungrammaticality of sentences such as (23) may be accounted for by the *i*-within-*i* Condition along the lines discussed in the previous section.

When *ne* and *personne* are in different clauses, as in (24), *personne* can appear only in object position:

(24)
a. ?Jean n'exige   que Pierre voit personne
   Jean neg requires that Pierre sees body
   'Jean (neg) requires Pierre to see nobody'

b. *Jean n'exige   que personne vienne
   Jean neg requires that body   comes
   'Jean requires nobody to come'

We have accounted for this subject-object asymmetry by assuming with R. S. Kayne (1981c) that *personne* undergoes Quantifier-Raising in LF and that *ne* is a scope marker indicating the clause to which *personne* is raised. The LF representations of (24a–b) will be as follows:

(25)
a. [personne]$_i$ Jean n'exige que Pierre voit x_i
b. [personne]$_i$ Jean n'exige que x_i vienne

(25b), which contains a non–properly governed variable, will be ruled out by the ECP or by the generalized binding theory. The contrast between (25a) and (25b) is similar to the one between (26a) and (26b):

(26)
a. who$_i$ do you think that John saw x_i
b. who$_i$ do you think that x_i left

In this sense, it is possible to say that *personne* is treated as a variable.

However, there exists another dialect in French where *personne* is treated not as a variable but as an anaphor that must be related to *ne*. In this dialect, analyzed in Milner 1979, the distribution of *personne* is similar to that of reciprocals and reflexives. In particular, both (24a) and (24b) will be ruled out by the binding theory, since *personne* does not have an antecedent in its governing category, the embedded clause.

On the other hand, neither (22a–b) nor (27a–b) will violate the binding theory, since *personne* is bound in its governing category by *ne:*

(27)

a. Jean requiert que Pierre ne voit personne
   Jean requires that Pierre neg sees body
   'Jean requires Pierre to see nobody'

b. Jean requiert que personne ne voit Pierre
   Jean requires that body   neg sees Pierre
   'Jean requires nobody to see Pierre'

These two sentences will also be grammatical in the dialect analyzed by Kayne. In the dialect where *personne* is treated as an anaphor, the antecedent of *personne*—namely, *ne*—is not in an A-position. Thus, the relation between *ne* and *personne* illustrates another instance of an $\bar{\text{A}}$-anaphoric relation: *ne* is the $\bar{\text{A}}$-antecedent of *personne*.

With respect to the generalized binding theory, the difference between the two dialects may be characterized as follows: in the dialect where *personne* is treated as a variable (dialect A), *personne* is subject to principles (A) and (C) of the binding theory; in the dialect where *personne* is treated as an anaphor (dialect B), it will be subject only to principle (A). To see the difference between the two dialects in terms of the generalized binding theory, consider the simplified representations (28a–b):

(28)

a. Jean AGR n'exige [$_{\bar{\text{S}}}$ que Pierre AGR voit personne]

b. Jean AGR n'exige [$_{\bar{\text{S}}}$ que personne vienne]

Consider first the behavior of *personne* in dialect (A). In (28a) *personne* has no accessible SUBJECT: neither AGR of the embedded clause nor AGR of the matrix clause can function as accessible SUBJECT; their doing so would violate binding principle (C). Therefore, the root clause will count as the governing category for the governed *personne*, which lacks an accessible SUBJECT. In this governing category, *personne* is $\bar{\text{A}}$-bound by *ne*. In (28b) AGR of the embedded clause counts as a SUBJECT accessible to *personne*; the minimal maximal projection containing this SUBJECT will be the embedded clause, which is therefore the governing category for *personne*. In this category *personne* is free, thus violating the binding theory. Therefore, (28b) is ungrammatical.

Now consider the behavior of *personne* in dialect (B). In both (28a) and (28b) the SUBJECT accessible to *personne* is AGR of the embedded clause. Therefore, the embedded clause will count as the governing category for *personne*. In this category *personne* is free, thus violating the binding theory. Both sentences are ungrammatical in this dialect.

The generalized binding theory excludes the existence of a "mixed dialect" where (28b) is grammatical and (28a) is not. Three other dialects may potentially occur:

(29)
a. Dialect (A): (28a) is grammatical, (28b) ungrammatical
                  (the subject-object asymmetry)
b. Dialect (B): both (28a) and (28b) are ungrammatical
c. Dialect (C): both (28a) and (28b) are grammatical
d. *Dialect (D): (28a) is ungrammatical, (28b) grammatical

As we have seen, in dialect (A) *personne* functions as an anaphor and a namelike expression and as such will be subject to binding principles (A) and (C). In dialect (B) *personne* is treated as an anaphor; it will be subject only to principle (A). In both dialects the relation between *ne* and *personne* is a binding relation: *ne* $\bar{\text{A}}$-binds *personne*. In dialect (C), however, the relation between *ne* and *personne* is not a binding relation: *ne* neither A-binds nor $\bar{\text{A}}$-binds *personne*. In this dialect *personne* may be characterized as a "polarity item" that appears in specific contexts—a negative one, for instance. That is why it must cooccur with *ne* (see Milner 1979 for more details). In other words, in dialect (C) *personne* is treated as a namelike expression only; it will be subject to binding principle (C).[2] This dialect seems to exist in Spanish; there are speakers for whom *ninguno* may have matrix scope in configurations corresponding to (28a–b) (see the discussion of (10)).

This discussion concerning *personne* may have interesting consequences. Even though *personne* in dialect (A) displays the standard subject-object asymmetry, its behavior may be accounted for without postulating an LF movement rule. Might this account extend to *wh*-in-situ (i.e., to a *wh*-element that has not undergone Move α in Syntax)? Consider the following contrast:

(30)
a. I don't remember which man said that John saw which woman
b. ?*I don't remember which man said that which woman saw John

This contrast may be accounted for by the ECP or by the generalized binding theory if it is assumed that Move α in LF raises the *wh*-in-situ *which woman* to the COMP containing *which man*. It follows from the generalized binding theory that a variable in object position does not have an accessible SUBJECT, whereas a variable in the subject position of a tensed clause has an accessible SUBJECT—the AGR element of this clause. Consequently, the governing category for the variable in object position will be the root clause, and the governing category for the variable in subject position will be the tensed clause of which it is the subject:

(31)
a. $[_{\bar{S}^*}$ I don't remember [which woman$_j$ which man$_i$ $[x_i$ said that John saw $x_j]]]$
b. $[_{\bar{S}}$ I don't remember $[_{\bar{S}}$ which woman$_j$ which man$_i$ $[x_i$ said $[_{\bar{S}^*}$ that x_j saw John]]]]]$
   (where * indicates the governing category)

The variable x_j in (31a)—but not in (31b)—is $\bar{A}$-bound in its governing category. (31b) will be excluded by the binding theory (see chapter 2 for more details).

The assumption that Move α in LF raises the *wh*-element is not crucial. The *wh*-in-situ is raised to a COMP marked [+wh]—that is, in general to a COMP already filled by a *wh*-element.[3] Let us assume that the COMP marked [+wh] is the $\bar{A}$-binder of the *wh*-in-situ and that the *wh*-in-situ is subject to principles (A) and (C) of the binding theory. In other words, the *wh*-in-situ will behave like *personne* in dialect (A). In particular, it will display the standard subject-object asymmetry that characterizes elements subject to principles (A) and (C). Obviously, these considerations do not show that Move α in LF does not exist. Rather, they indicate that the subject-object asymmetry does not force us to postulate an LF movement rule. It can in fact be accounted for in a framework that dispenses with LF movement, such as the one proposed in Van Riemsdijk and Williams 1981.

5.3 Binding and Quantification

We have seen that the generalized binding theory accounts for the behavior of negative *personne* in Romance. In this section we will see that it also accounts for the different scope properties of quantifiers.[4]

5.3.1 A Typology of Quantifiers

Consider the following sentences:

(32)
a. someone believes that everyone likes cars
b. someone believes that Frank likes everyone

In these sentences the matrix quantified NP has wide scope over the quantified phrase in the embedded clause: *someone* is interpreted as having scope over *everyone*. These quantifier dependencies will follow if the LF representations of (32a–b) are (33a–b), respectively, and not (34a–b):

(33)
a. [someone x] x believes that [everyone y] y likes cars
b. [someone x] x believes that [everyone y] Frank likes y

(34)
a. *[everyone y] [someone x] x believes that y likes cars
b. *[everyone y] [someone x] x believes that Frank likes y

In (33a–b) *someone* c-commands *everyone* and thus is interpreted as having scope over *everyone*, whereas in (34a–b) it is *everyone* that c-commands, and hence has scope over, *everyone*. More generally, as indicated in May 1977, quantification seems clause-bound: Quantifier-Raising seems to append a moved quantified NP only to a position within the most proximate clause.

However, there seem to be quantifiers that do not obey this generalization. A clear instance is *ne . . . personne* in the dialect where *personne* is treated as a variable, namely, dialect (A) of (29). Another is *wh*-in-situ. These elements are subject to Move α in LF: they are attached to a COMP containing a [+wh] element even though this COMP is not in the same clause $\overline{S}$ as the *wh*-in-situ. This type of quantifier, which is not clause-bound, displays a subject-object asymmetry accounted for by the generalized binding theory under the assumption that these elements are subject to binding principles (A) and (C).

A situation similar to that of dialect (A) where *personne* is treated as a variable occurs in English, as indicated in Kayne 1981c. Kayne points out that only in examples such as (35a) may *not a single* have a wide-scope interpretation:

(35)
a. in all these weeks, he's suggested that they write not a single paper
b. in all these weeks, he's suggested that not a single paper be written

Once again this subject-object asymmetry characteristic of the ECP may be accounted for in our terms by the generalized binding theory.

ECP effects also occur with the so-called clause-bound quantifiers, as illustrated in sentences such as (36a–b) (first pointed out by N. Chomsky):

(36)
a. someone expects that everyone will be elected
b. someone expects everyone to be elected

In (36b), but not in (36a), the embedded quantifier may have scope over the matrix quantifier. This is because the variable in (36b), but not the one in (36a), will be in a position properly governed by the matrix verb if *everyone* is raised to the matrix clause. (37a–b) correspond to the wide-scope interpretation of *everyone* in (36a–b):

(37)
a. *[everyone y] [someone x] [x expects that y will be elected]
b. [everyone y] [someone x] [x expects y to be elected]

Strictly speaking, (37b) violates the generalization concerning the clause-boundedness of *everyone* if clauses are taken to be S rather than $\bar{\text{S}}$. (We will return to the significance of these facts.)

There exists a third type of quantifier that, although non-clause-bound, displays no subject-object asymmetry; that is, it shows no ECP effect. Consider (38), for instance:

(38)
John does not believe that anyone likes bagels

Any is traditionally treated as a universal quantifier taking wide scope. The LF representation of (38) would thus be (39):

(39)
[$\forall x$: x is a person] John does not believe that x likes bagels

This representation should involve a violation of the ECP. Nevertheless, it is fully acceptable. *Any* behaves differently from other quantifiers not only with respect to the ECP but also with respect to the weak crossover phenomenon, in that it does not display weak crossover effects (Chomsky 1977a, Higginbotham 1980):

(40)

a. that he might be laughed at won't bother anyone

b. that he might be laughed at won't bother John

c. *that he might be laughed at won't bother everyone

Furthermore, unlike other quantifiers, *any* may bind a pronoun without c-commanding it:

(41)

a. if John finds any dog, he beats it

b. if John finds Fido, he beats it

c. *if John finds every dog, he beats it

As argued in Aoun, Hornstein, and Sportiche 1981 and Hornstein 1981a,b, the behavior of *any* is similar to the behavior of names. Like names, *any* will not be subject to the ECP, will not display weak crossover effects, and will not need to c-command a pronoun in order to bind it.

The following picture emerges. There are three types of quantifiers. The first is not clause-bound, the second is. Both of these types obey the ECP. The third type is not clause-bound and does not obey the ECP (see Hornstein 1981a,b):

(42)

a. Type I quantifiers: not clause-bound, obey the ECP (*wh*-in-situ, *not a single, personne* in dialects where it is treated as a variable, etc.)

b. Type II quantifiers: "clause-bound," obey the ECP (*everyone, someone,* etc.)

c. Type III quantifiers: not clause-bound, do not obey the ECP (*any, a certain,* etc.)

The behavior of the three types of quantifiers essentially parallels the behavior of the three *ne . . . personne* dialects discussed in section 5.2. The behavior of type I quantifiers, like the behavior of *personne* in dialect (A), is accounted for by assuming that they are subject to binding principles (A) and (C). Type III quantifiers behave like names: they are subject to binding principle (C). In this respect they behave like *personne* in dialect (C).

As for type II quantifiers, they behave like *personne* in dialect (B) in being subject only to binding principle (A). The so-called ECP effect displayed by type II in (37a–b) (repeated here) is straightforwardly accounted for by assuming that type II quantifiers are subject to this principle:

(37)
a. *[everyone y] [someone x] [x expects that y will be elected]
b. [everyone y] [someone x] [x expects y to be elected]

Claiming that a type II quantifier is subject only to binding principle (A) amounts to claiming that the contrast between (37a) and (37b) parallels the contrast between (43a) and (43b):

(43)
a. *John$_i$ expects that himself$_i$ will be elected
b. John$_i$ expects himself$_i$ to be elected

The anaphor *himself* in (43) and the empty category left by the type II quantifier in (37) are subject to binding principle (A). The empty category y in (37a) and the anaphor *himself* in (43a) are free in their governing category, which is the embedded clause: it is the minimal clause containing an accessible SUBJECT, namely, AGR of the embedded clause. Therefore, (37a) and (43a) violate binding principle (A).

Now consider (37b) and (43b). The governing category for the anaphors y in (37b) and *himself* in (43b) is the matrix clause, since the nonfinite embedded clause lacks an accessible SUBJECT. These anaphors are bound in this governing category: the empty category y is $\bar{\text{A}}$-bound by *everyone,* and the reflexive *himself* is A-bound by *John.* Binding principle (A) is not violated. In short, the so-called ECP contrast illustrated in (37a–b) is accounted for by principle (A) of the binding theory.

We have thus accomplished the goal of this section: to show the parallelism between the three types of quantifiers and the three *ne . . . personne* dialects in Romance and to argue that it can be accounted for by the generalized binding theory:

a. Dialect (A) of (29) is parallel to type I quantifiers of (42). Both are subject to principles (A) and (C) of the binding theory.
b. Dialect (B) of (29) is parallel to type II quantifiers of (42). Both are subject to principle (A) of the binding theory.
c. Dialect (C) of (29) is parallel to type III quantifiers of (42). Both are subject to principle (C) of the binding theory.

5.3.2 The *i*-within-*i* Condition and the Binding Principles

Other aspects of the present analysis concern the *i*-within-*i* Condition on well-formedness. For type II quantifiers, binding principle (A) requires the empty category left by their LF extraction to be $\bar{A}$-bound in its governing category. The *i*-within-*i* Condition is relevant to the notion "accessible SUBJECT" that enters into the definition of governing category (section 2.3.2). However, it is not relevant to type II quantifiers, as the following examples illustrate:

(44)

a. they$_i$ AGR said that [$_{NP_k}$ pictures of each other$_i$] AGR$_k$ would be on sale

b. they$_i$ AGR said that [$_{NP_k}$ pictures of them$_i$] AGR$_k$ would be on sale

In a representation such as (44a) the governing category for the reciprocal is the matrix clause: being coindexed with the subject, AGR of the embedded clause is not accessible to *each other;* AGR of the matrix clause, however, is. The reciprocal is bound in the matrix clause, and the sentence is grammatical. As discussed in section 2.4.2, C.-T. J. Huang (1982) argues that for binding principle (B), which constrains pronouns, the *i*-within-*i* Condition is irrelevant. Thus, in (44b) the governing category for the pronoun is the embedded clause, in which it is free. Thus, nothing prevents this pronoun from being coindexed with an element outside its governing category, such as the subject of the matrix clause. Now consider the following contrast:

(45)

a. someone took [$_{NP}$ a picture of everyone]

b. someone thought that [$_{NP}$ a picture of everyone] was pretty

In (45a) *everyone* may have scope wider or narrower than *someone*. In (45b), on the other hand, *everyone* cannot have scope over *someone;* it is not ambiguous. The LF representation of the wide-scope reading of (45b) is as follows:

(46)

[everyone y] [someone x] [x AGR thought that [$_{NP}$ a picture of y] AGR was pretty]

According to the *i*-within-*i* Condition, AGR of the embedded clause should not be accessible to y. The first accessible SUBJECT should be AGR of the matrix clause. (46) should be a well-formed representation because y would be bound in its governing category, the matrix clause, by *everyone*. We therefore expect the wide-scope reading of *everyone* to be available in (45b). But this is not the case.

In the dialects where *personne* is treated as an anaphor, however, the *i*-within-*i* Condition is relevant:

(47)
?je n'exige que [la photo de personne] soit sur la table
'I (neg) require the picture of no one to be on the table'

The governing category for *personne* is the matrix clause: AGR of the embedded clause is not accessible to *personne* because it is coindexed with the subject containing *personne*. In this governing category *personne* is bound by *ne*. ((47) is also discussed in note 1.)

It thus appears that for principle (A) the *i*-within-*i* Condition is relevant to elements that have an overt antecedent: reciprocals, reflexives, *ne . . . personne*. But it is not relevant to elements such as the trace left by raised quantifiers. This indicates that we must extend Huang's remarks concerning the *i*-within-*i* Condition: whereas he claims that this condition is relevant to principle (A) but not to principle (B), we have seen that for principle (A) it is relevant only to elements that have an overt binder.

We can now suggest the following generalization: the *i*-within-*i* Condition is relevant only to elements that have an overt binder. As pointed out in Lasnik 1976, 1981, for a pronoun to be interpreted as coreferential with another element, we need not coindex this pronoun with the coreferential element. We need only a disjoint reference rule that prevents a pronoun in certain contexts from being construed as coreferential with another element. This disjoint reference rule is nothing more than binding principle (B). This being the case, an automatic consequence of our generalization about overt binders is that the *i*-within-*i* Condition will be irrelevant to pronouns—that is, to principle (B) of the binding theory. For principle (A), it will be relevant only to elements with an overt antecedent.[5]

Thus, there are three types of quantifiers; their behavior is accounted for by the generalized binding theory, which incorporates the notion of A̅-anaphor. Insofar as this theory provides a unified account for the distribution of these quantifiers and for the parallelism between them and *ne . . . personne* constructions in Romance, its empirical and explanatory adequacy is confirmed.

5.4 Overt $\overline{\text{A}}$-Anaphors with No Independent θ-Role

Anaphoric elements may be overt or not and may bear an independent θ-role or not. With respect to this classification, *personne*—in the dialects where this element is subject to binding principle (A)—is an overt $\overline{\text{A}}$-anaphor with an independent θ-role. We will now examine overt $\overline{\text{A}}$-anaphors that do not bear an independent θ-role.

Like A-anaphors, $\overline{\text{A}}$-anaphors may be characterized with respect to the features [$\pm\theta$-role], [$\pm$overt]. I repeat the matrix from the beginning of the chapter:

(1)
$\overline{\text{A}}$-anaphors
a. [$+\theta$-role, $+$overt] : reciprocals in Italian
b. [$-\theta$-role, $+$overt] :
c. [$-\theta$-role, $-$overt] : clitic-trace
d. [$+\theta$-role, $-$overt] : *wh*-trace

We have discussed cases (1a), (1c), and (1d) in chapters 1, 2, and 3–4, respectively. Let us now turn to case (1b). Consider the following sentences:

(48)
a. there is a book on the table
b. what$_i$ is there x_i on the table

As indicated in Milsark 1974, 1977 and Safir 1982, in existential constructions such as (48) a definiteness restriction is at work that prevents *there* from cooccurring with a definite NP:[6]

(49)
*there is the book on the table

As a consequence of this restriction, *there* always cooccurs either with an indefinite NP, as in (48), or with a quantified NP, as in (50):[7]

(50)
a. there is no book on the table
b. there isn't any book on the table

Assuming that indefinite NPs, like quantified NPs, undergo the LF rule of Quantifier-Raising, the LF representation of sentences like (48a), for instance, will look like (51):

(51)
QP$_i$ [there is x_i ...]

In GB theory *there* and the postverbal NP form a chain; the motivation of this assumption was discussed in section 2.10. Being in the same chain with the postverbal NP, *there* will bear the same index as this NP. Thus, a more accurate representation than (51) is (52). (This discussion is directly influenced by Safir 1982, although it differs in some respects from the proposal suggested there.)

(52)
QP$_i$ [there$_i$ is x_i ...]

In (52) *there* is coindexed with an element in an $\bar{\text{A}}$-position, namely, the raised QP; it is $\bar{\text{A}}$-bound by this QP. I would like to suggest that *there* is an $\bar{\text{A}}$-anaphor. Obviously, it is the postverbal element and not *there* itself that bears the θ-role assumed by the whole chain. This being the case, *there* will be an overt $\bar{\text{A}}$-anaphor that does not bear an independent θ-role, thus instantiating case (1b).

The assumption that *there* is an $\bar{\text{A}}$-anaphor may help to explain why it must be obligatorily lowered. In section 3.1 we argued that *there* must be lowered in LF to its base-generated position and that the output of this lowering process is subject to the binding theory. This proposal accounted for the ungrammaticality of constructions containing doubly raised *there*, as in (53):

(53)
?*there seems to be likely to be someone in the room

In existential constructions such as (54) *there* and the postverbal NP, although constituting a chain, do not enter into a binding relation; if they did, the binding theory would be violated:

(54)
there is a man in the room

In LGB (chapter 6), it is suggested that a special indexing mechanism that is not relevant for binding is at work between *there* and the postverbal NP. This indexing mechanism is referred to as *superscripting:* in (54) *there* and the postverbal NP are cosuperscripted and not cosubscripted. In Rizzi 1982a and in Safir 1982 (where cosuperscripting is dispensed with) other proposals are discussed. For our purposes, it suffices to bear in mind that no binding relation is at work between

there and the postverbal NP. However, when *there* itself is raised, as in
(55), the empty category left by this extraction enters into a binding
relation with *there*. In terms of LGB, it is subscripted with the antecedent *there:*

(55)
[there$_i$ seems [t_i to be someone in the room]]

In LF, Quantifier-Raising may adjoin *someone* to the matrix or the
embedded clause:

(56)
a. [someone$_j$ [there$_i$ seems [t_i to be x_j in the room]]]
b. [there$_i$ seems [someone$_j$ [t_i to be x_j in the room]]]

In (56b) the ($\overline{A}$)-anaphoric *there* is not bound by *someone* because it is
not in the scope of this quantifier. In (56a) it cannot be $\overline{A}$-bound by
someone for slightly more complicated reasons. Let us assume that
someone in (56a) $\overline{A}$-binds *there*. In this case *someone* and the chain
(*there*, *t*) will bear the same index. For the sake of simplicity, we will
consider that $i = j$:

(57)
[someone$_j$ [there$_j$ seems [t_j to be x_j in the room]]]

According to the functional characterization of empty categories, x in
(57) is identified as an NP-trace bound by *t* and *t* as an NP-trace bound
by *there*. Finally, *there* is $\overline{A}$-bound by *someone*. There are many ways
to rule out a representation such as (57). We might appeal to the θ-Cri-
terion: no element in the chain (*there*, *t*, *x*) can bear the θ-role assigned
in the embedded clause. Alternatively, we might appeal to the constraint ruling out representations containing a vacuous quantifier (i.e., a
quantifier that does not bind an appropriate variable (Chomsky 1982)):
in (57) no element would qualify as an appropriate variable. In brief,
when *there* has not been lowered to its base-generated position, no
well-formed LF derivation is possible.

   Now consider representations where *there* has been lowered in LF to
its base-generated position. (58) is the LF representation of (55) after
Lowering:

(58)
NP seems there to be someone in the room

Here too, the quantifier may be attached to the matrix or the embedded clause:

(59)
a. [someone$_i$ [NP seems [there to be x_i in the room]]]
b. NP seems [someone$_i$ [there to be x_i in the room]]

Since *there* and the postverbal NP do not enter into a binding relation, nothing in these sentences prevents *someone* from $\overline{A}$-binding *there*. The discussion of the contrast between (56)–(57) on the one hand and (59a–b) on the other amounts to saying that extraction is relevant to the binding theory: it creates a potential binding relation. Although the instantiation of this idea in constructions containing *there* seems complicated, the idea itself is uncontroversial in a framework where NP-traces are subject to the binding theory.

The proposal that existential constructions illustrate the case of a [+overt, −θ-role] $\overline{A}$-anaphor helps to explain why *there* must be lowered to its base-generated position. Another consequence of this proposal concerns the binding theory. We have seen that the binding theory applies at S-structure and LF. However, in sentences like (60), *there* is not $\overline{A}$-bound by the quantifier until LF unless it is assumed that the postverbal quantifier is already in an $\overline{A}$-position c-commanding *there:*

(60)
there is someone in the room

Let us assume that *there* is $\overline{A}$-bound at LF only. Given that the generalized binding theory refers to two separate binding relations (A-binding and $\overline{A}$-binding) and that A-indexing (but not $\overline{A}$-indexing) applies in Syntax, we can assume that only A-relations are checked at S-structure; in other words, that at S-structure the binding theory is a theory of A-binding and that at LF it is a theory of X-binding (A- and $\overline{A}$-binding). This will allow $\overline{A}$-anaphors such as *there* to be $\overline{A}$-free at S-structure without violating the binding principles.

5.5 The Position of Anaphors

Throughout this book we have characterized an A-anaphor as an anaphor that must be related to an antecedent in an A-position and an $\overline{A}$-anaphor as an anaphor that must be related to an antecedent in an $\overline{A}$-position. However, we have not discussed the position of the anaphor itself, which is usually considered to be an A-position. I would like to suggest that the anaphor itself may be in either an A-position or an $\bar{\text{A}}$-position.

Almost all the constructions discussed so far involve anaphors that are in an A-position. For example, in (61) the reflexive is in an object position:

(61)
John$_i$ likes himself$_i$

We have argued that clitics are in $\bar{\text{A}}$-positions. They may be pronouns subject to principle (B) of the binding theory, as in (62), or anaphors subject to principle (A), as in (63):

(62)
Jean$_i$ le$_j$ voit
'Jean sees him'

(63)
a. Jean$_i$ se$_i$ voit
   'Jean sees himself'
b. ce livre$_i$ se$_i$ vend bien
   'this book sells (itself) well'

In (63a) se is an overt anaphor with an independent θ-role; in (63b) it is an overt anaphor with no independent θ-role. Since clitics are in $\bar{\text{A}}$-positions and since they may be anaphoric, the grammar contains an instance of an anaphor in an $\bar{\text{A}}$-position.

Another such instance is illustrated by reciprocal constructions in Italian, discussed in section 1.1. Two anaphoric relations are at work in these constructions: (R1) (the anaphoric relation between l'uno and l'altro) and (R2) (the anaphoric relation between l'uno and an antecedent). These anaphoric relations hold when l'uno is in an $\bar{\text{A}}$-position. Since l'uno is in an $\bar{\text{A}}$-position and since for (R2) l'uno itself is an anaphor that must be related to an antecedent, l'uno is another instance of an anaphor in an $\bar{\text{A}}$-position.

Finally, consider floated quantifiers, which occur to the right of the NP they are related to:

(64)

a. i miei amici hanno parlato tutti dello stesso problema
   'my friends spoke all of the same problem'
b. *Mario ha parlato tutti dello stesso problema
   'Mario spoke all of the same problem'
c. Mario sostenne che i miei amici parlarono tutti dello stesso problema
   'Mario maintained that my friends spoke all of the same problem'
d. *i miei amici sostennero che Mario parlò tutti dello stesso problema
   'my friends maintained that Mario spoke all of the same problem'
e. *i miei amici mi hanno costretto a parlare tutti dello stesso problema
   'my friends obliged me to speak all of the same problem'
f. ho costretto i miei amici a parlare tutti dello stesso problema
   'I obliged my friends to speak all of the same problem'

As indicated in Kayne 1981a and Belletti 1982, the distribution of these quantifiers in English, French, and Italian may be accounted for if it is assumed that they are anaphoric. As such, they must be related to an antecedent in their governing category. In (64a–f) the anaphor is *tutti*. If the antecedent *i miei amici* occurs in the governing category of *tutti,* the sentences will be grammatical ((64a), (64c), and (64f)). If this antecedent is not in the governing category of *tutti,* however, the sentences will be excluded by the binding theory, since the anaphoric *tutti* will be left free ((64b), (64d), and (64e)).

Clearly, the floated quantifier *tutti* in (64a–f), which we have seen to be an anaphor, is not in an A-position. It is therefore a third instance of an anaphor in an Ā-position.

5.6 Conclusion

In this book I have suggested the existence of two anaphoric systems: the A-anaphoric system and the Ā-anaphoric system. Anaphors belonging to the A-anaphoric system are related to an antecedent in an A-position, and anaphors belonging to the Ā-anaphoric system are related to an antecedent in an Ā-position. Both anaphoric systems are constrained by the binding theory, which must be generalized to constrain both A- and Ā-anaphoric relations. The anaphoric systems are symmetric: for each type of A-anaphor, there exists a corresponding Ā-anaphor. As for the anaphoric expression itself, it may occur in either an A-position or an Ā-position.

Notes

Chapter 2

1. Later, the assumption concerning covert subjects will turn out to be unnecessary. G. Cinque (1980) and D. Steriade (1980) also indicate that the same seems to hold for clitic movement out of the NP: only subjects can be extracted from an NP and cliticized to a verb. We will return to this observation in this chapter and in chapter 3. Empty elements left by cliticization will be (partially) assimilated to variables; like variables, they are $\overline{A}$-bound elements.

2. For some speakers, (13) seems marginal. The Specificity Constraint, which prohibits a free variable inside an NP (Fiengo and Higginbotham 1981), is presumably to be invoked.

3. R. S. Kayne (1975) records examples like (i) as grammatical:

(i)
elles vont souvent dans les chambres les unes des autres
'they often go to each other's rooms'

In all accounts, the contrast between (i) and (69) is left unexplained. Sentence (i) does not seem to be representative in Romance languages, however, as will become clear when we discuss the distribution of reciprocals in NPs in Italian, which is similar to that of reciprocals in French.

4. As indicated in Belletti 1982, a sentence such as (2b) of section 1.1, repeated in (i), is worse than a sentence such as (72):

(i)
*hanno criticato [$_{NP}$ le idee dell'uno l'altro]
'they criticized the ideas of each other'

In (72) only the binding requirement is violated. In (i) two violations occur: a violation of the binding requirement—the A-anaphor *l'uno* is free in the NP—and a violation of the nonadjacency requirement between *l'uno* and *l'altro* discussed in section 1.1.

Chapter 4

1. See Kayne 1975, Rouveret and Vergnaud 1980 (henceforth SRS). The content of this presentation is from SRS. Most of the modifications are a restatement of Rouveret and Vergnaud's analysis in the framework we are assuming.

2. For expository purposes I will informally distinguish between opaque and transparent subjects. Roughly speaking, the subject of a clause α is *opaque* when it prevents an element in α from being related to an element outside α; it is transparent otherwise. Thus, in (17c) the subject of the embedded clause (*à Pierre*) is opaque because it prevents the cliticization of y onto the matrix verb. In (17d) the cliticized subject (*leur*) is transparent because it does not prevent the cliticization of y.

3. In order to accommodate cases such as (i) where the clitic is related to the complement position of *portrait*,

(i)
Jean en$_i$ a vu [$_{NP}$ le   portrait e_i]
Jean of him saw   the portrait
'Jean saw the portrait of him'

it is necessary to extend the characterization of "dependent of" as follows: α is a *dependent of β* iff α is governed by β or the first maximal projection dominating α is governed by β. This recalls the notions of c-subjacency or c′-command given in SRS. Alternatively, recall that in section 2.6 we assumed that the subject of the NP in Romance is coindexed with the prenominal position. If the prenominal position is accessible to government by the verb, it will be possible to assume that e in (i) is governed by the verb via the prenominal position. This is another case of indirect government such as the one discussed below in the text in (44). The prenominal position itself will be accessible to government by the verb if, as suggested in Vergnaud (forthcoming), the prenominal (Specifier) position is the head of the NP: as indicated in Belletti and Rizzi 1981, if an element α is governed by β, the head of α will be governed by β.

4. Obviously, the two solutions are not incompatible. That is, AGR may be in a separate chain from the one containing the subject, and the variable in subject position may be in a separate chain from the one containing the *wh*-element in COMP.

5. Recall from chapter 2 that $\bar{S}$ and not S is to be taken as the governing category. However, in (57b) and in (i), where $\bar{S}$-Deletion occurs, we must consider that the embedded clause is the governing category for the reciprocal:

(i)
*they believe [$_{S_1}$[$_{S_0}$ John to have seen each other]]

To reconcile this with the assumption that $\bar{S}$ and not S is to be taken as the governing category, it is possible to view the so-called $\bar{S}$-Deletion process (section 2.9) as an $\bar{S}$-Transparency process marking an $\bar{S}$ transparent with respect to the verb triggering this process.

6. This may be the case if such a peripheral position is in a different dimension from the one containing the matrix verb and the embedded clause. (See Halle and Vergnaud 1981 for a multidimensional approach to phonology and Vergnaud (forthcoming) for its application in Syntax.)

7. If the phrasal position after *seem* is treated as an A-position, it will be governed by *seem* and will receive its Case and its θ-role from *seem*. If it is treated as an Ā-position, it will receive neither its Case nor its θ-role from *seem*. Presumably, it will receive the same Case assigned to appositives. As for the θ-role, it is tempting to consider that it is the same as the one assigned in (i) to the clitic *te* in French (i.e., benefactive):

(i)
Pierre *te*   les   frappera
Pierre you them will hit
'Pierre will hit them for you'

8. For the notion of accessible chain discussed in this section, the *wh*-trace and its antecedent do not act as a single chain. This does not mean that for different principles, they do not act as a single chain. It would be plausible to assume that for purely logical principles where operator-binding is involved, the notion of Ā-chain will be relevant: the *wh*-trace and its antecedent form an Ā-chain.

Chapter 5

1. The same facts are illustrated in Italian (thanks to M.-R. Manzini):

(i)
a. *la foto   di nessuno è sul   tavolo
   the picture of no one   is on the table

b. non voglio la foto   di nessuno sul   tavolo
   neg (I) want the picture of no one on the table

In French, intuitions are obscured by the somewhat marginal character of the *ne . . . personne* constructions (see Kayne 1981c). It is therefore not surprising that judgments are more vague for (ii):

(ii)
?je n'exige   que la photo de personne soit sur la table
 I (neg) require that the picture of no one   be on the table

As pointed out to me by J.-C. Milner, the choice of the matrix verb seems to be relevant in French: (iii) is less acceptable than (ii):

(iii)
??je ne   crois que la photo de personne est sur la table
  I (neg) think that the picture of no one   is on the table

Nevertheless, he indicates that (iv) is worse than (ii) (cf. Milner 1979):

(iv)
*la   photo de personne n'est   sur la table
 the picture of no one   (neg) is on the table

R. S. Kayne has pointed out to me that *aucun* does not seem to behave like *personne:*

(v)
le sourire d'aucun garçon ne   m'accueillera   ce soir
the smile of no   boy   (neg) will welcome me tonight

However, according to the speakers I have consulted, (v) seems to have the same status as (iv) when *garçon* is omitted,

(vi)
*le sourire d'aucun   ne   m'accueillera   ce soir
 the smile   of no one (neg) will welcome me tonight

and it is possible to improve (iv) as in (vii):

(vii)
la   photo de personne d'autre n'est   sur la   table
the picture of no one   else   (neg) is on the table

In brief, (v) and (vii) are to be treated on a par and are to be contrasted with (iv) and (vi). It is possible to assume that *ne* is not coindexed with *personne* in (vii) or *aucun* in (v); hence, the *i*-within-*i* Condition will be irrelevant. I will suggest an explanation for the grammatical status of (v) and (vii) in note 2.

2. In note 1 we saw that (ia–b) are to be contrasted with (iia–b), which are unacceptable:

(i)
a. le sourire d'aucun garçon ne m'accueillera ce soir
   'the smile of no boy (neg) will welcome me tonight'
b. la photo de personne d'autre n'est sur la table
   'the picture of no one else (neg) is on the table'

(ii)
a. *le sourire d'aucun ne m'accueillera ce soir
b. *la photo de personne n'est sur la table

Since *ne* is coindexed neither with *aucun garçon* (ia) nor with *personne d'autre* (ib), the *i*-within-*i* Condition is irrelevant in these sentences. I would now suggest that the polarity items in (ia–b) are treated as namelike expressions subject only to principle (C) of the binding theory. If this suggestion is correct, we (for instance) expect these items not to display the standard subject-object asymmetry characteristic of elements that are subject to binding principles (A) and (C). This seems to be the case, as illustrated in (iii), which is to be contrasted with (24a–b):

(iii)
a. ?je n'exige que personne d'autre vienne
   'I (neg) require no one else to come'
b. ?je n'exige qu'aucun garçon ne vienne
   'I (neg) require no boy to come'

3. See Aoun, Hornstein, and Sportiche 1981 for languages such as French where syntactic *Wh*-Movement is optional:

(i)

Jean veut   que Pierre voit qui
Jean wants that Pierre sees who
'who does Jean want Pierre to see'

Roughly, it follows from this account that the matrix COMP counts as the [+wh] COMP in (i). Thus, the remarks in the text apply to languages such as French. (Also see Huang 1982.)

4. This section is based on a paper presented by N. Hornstein and myself at the thirteenth conference of the North Eastern Linguistic Society at the Université du Québec à Montréal.

5. D. Sportiche (1983) argues that the i-within-i Condition is not relevant to empty categories. In the text we have argued that it is relevant to elements with an overt antecedent. One way of reconciling the two results is to assume that the i-within-i Condition is relevant to overt elements that have an overt antecedent.

6. It goes without saying that *there* in existential constructions is to be distinguished from locative *there*, as in (ia–b):

(i)

a. there is the table
b. John is there

7. This does not mean that any quantified NP may cooccur with *there*. This is illustrated by (i), the ungrammaticality of which is discussed in Safir 1982:

(i)
*there is every book on the table

References

Aissen, J., and D. Perlmutter (1976). Clause reduction in Spanish. In *Proceedings of the Second Annual Meeting of the Berkeley Linguistics Society*. University of California at Berkeley.

Anderson, S., and P. Kiparsky, eds. (1973). *A Festschrift for Morris Halle*. New York: Holt, Rinehart and Winston.

Aoun, J. (1979). On government, Case-marking and clitic placement. Ms., Massachusetts Institute of Technology.

Aoun, J. (1981a). ECP, Move α, and Subjacency. *Linguistic Inquiry* 12.4.

Aoun, J. (1981b). *The Formal Nature of Anaphoric Relations*. Doctoral dissertation, Massachusetts Institute of Technology.

Aoun, J. (1982). Expletive PROs. In *MIT Working Papers in Linguistics* 4. Department of Linguistics and Philosophy, Massachusetts Institute of Technology.

Aoun, J. (to appear). *Generalized Binding*. Dordrecht: Foris Publications.

Aoun, J., N. Hornstein, and D. Sportiche (1981). Some aspects of wide scope quantifications. *Journal of Linguistic Research* 1.3.

Aoun, J., and D. Sportiche (1983). On the formal theory of government. *The Linguistic Review* 2.3.

Aoun, J., D. Sportiche, J.-R. Vergnaud, and M.-L. Zubizaretta (1980). Reconstruction and logical form. Ms., Massachusetts Institute of Technology.

Belletti, A. (1982). On the anaphoric status of the reciprocal constructions in Italian. *The Linguistic Review* 2.2.

Belletti, A., and L. Rizzi (1981). The syntax of *ne:* Some theoretical implications. *The Linguistic Review* 1.2.

Bordelois, I. (1974). *The Grammar of Spanish Causative Complements*. Doctoral dissertation, Massachusetts Institute of Technology.

Borer, H. (1979). Restrictive relatives in Modern Hebrew. Ms., Massachusetts Institute of Technology.

Borer, H. (1984). *Parametric Syntax*. Dordrecht: Foris Publications.

Bouchard, D. (1984). *On the Content of Empty Categories*. Dordrecht: Foris Publications.

Brody, M. (1982). Anaphoric dependencies and conditions on domains. Paper presented at the 1982 GLOW conference, Paris.

Burzio, L. (1981). *Intransitive Verbs and Italian Auxiliaries*. Doctoral dissertation, Massachusetts Institute of Technology. (To be published by D. Reidel, Dordrecht.)

Chomsky, N. (1970). Remarks on nominalization. In R. A. Jacobs and P. S. Rosenbaum, eds., *Readings in English Transformational Grammar*. Waltham, Mass.: Ginn. (Also in Chomsky (1972).)

Chomsky, N. (1972). *Studies on Semantics in Generative Grammar*. The Hague: Mouton.

Chomsky, N. (1973). Conditions on transformations. In S. R. Anderson and P. Kiparsky, eds., *A Festschrift for Morris Halle*. New York: Holt, Rinehart and Winston.

Chomsky, N. (1977a). *Essays on Form and Interpretation*. Amsterdam: North Holland.

Chomsky, N. (1977b). On wh-movement. In P. Culicover, T. Wasow, and A. Akmajian, eds., *Formal Syntax*. New York: Academic Press.

Chomsky, N. (1979). *The Pisa Lectures*. Transcripts of lectures given at the 1979 GLOW conference, Scuola Normale Superiore, Pisa.

Chomsky, N. (1980) (OB). On binding. *Linguistic Inquiry* 11.1.

Chomsky, N. (1981) (LGB). *Lectures on Government and Binding*. Dordrecht: Foris Publications.

Chomsky, N. (1982). *Some Concepts and Consequences of the Theory of Government and Binding*. Cambridge, Mass.: The MIT Press.

Cinque, G. (1980). On extraction from NP in Italian. *Journal of Italian Linguistics* 5.1/2.

Dresher, B. E., and N. Hornstein (1979). Trace theory and NP movement rules. *Linguistic Inquiry* 10.1.

Emonds, J. (1976). *A Transformational Approach to English Syntax*. New York: Academic Press.

Engdahl, E. (1983). Parasitic gaps. *Linguistics and Philosophy* 6.1.

Fiengo, R., and J. Higginbotham (1981). Opacity in NP. *Linguistic Analysis* 7.4.

Freidin, R., and H. Lasnik (1981). Disjoint reference and *wh*-trace. *Linguistic Inquiry* 12.1.

George, L. (1980). *Analogical Generalizations of Natural Language Syntax.* Doctoral dissertation, Massachusetts Institute of Technology.

Godard, D. (1980). Les relatives complexes en français. Dissertation, Université de Paris VII.

Halle, M., and J.-R. Vergnaud (1981). Three dimensional phonology. *Journal of Linguistic Research* 1.1.

Higginbotham, J. (1980). Pronouns and bound variables. *Linguistic Inquiry* 11.4.

Higginbotham, J. (1983). Logical form, binding, and nominals. *Linguistic Inquiry* 14.3.

Hornstein, N. (1977). Towards a theory of tense. *Linguistic Inquiry* 8.3.

Hornstein, N. (1981a). The interpretation of natural language quantifiers. Ms., Columbia University.

Hornstein, N. (1981b). Two ways of interpreting quantifiers. Ms., Columbia University.

Hornstein, N., and A. Weinberg (1981). Preposition stranding and Case-marking. *Linguistic Inquiry* 12.1.

Huang, C.-T. J. (1982). *Logical Relations in Chinese and the Theory of Grammar.* Doctoral dissertation, Massachusetts Institute of Technology.

Jackendoff, R. (1977). *X̄-Syntax: A Study of Phrase Structure.* Cambridge, Mass.: The MIT Press.

Jaeggli, O. (1980). Remarks on *to* contraction. *Linguistic Inquiry* 11.1.

Jaeggli, O. (1982). *Topics in Romance Syntax.* Dordrecht: Foris Publications.

Kayne, R. S. (1975). *French Syntax.* Cambridge, Mass.: The MIT Press.

Kayne, R. S. (1981a). Binding, quantifiers, clitics and control. In F. Heny, ed., *Binding and Filtering.* Cambridge, Mass.: The MIT Press.

Kayne, R. S. (1981b). ECP extensions. *Linguistic Inquiry* 12.1.

Kayne, R. S. (1981c). Two notes on the NIC. In A. Belletti, L. Brandi, and L. Rizzi, eds., *Theory of Markedness in Generative Grammar.* Pisa: Scuola Normale Superiore.

Koopman, H. (1980). Resumptive pronouns in subject position. Ms., Université du Québec à Montréal.

Koopman, H. (1982). Theoretical implications of the distribution of *quoi.* In *Proceedings of the Twelfth Annual Meeting of the North Eastern Linguistics Society.* University of Massachusetts, Amherst.

Koopman, H., and D. Sportiche (1982). Variables and the Bijection Principle. *The Linguistic Review* 2.2.

Lasnik, H. (1976). Remarks on coreference. *Linguistic Analysis* 2.1.

Lasnik, H. (1981). On two recent treatments of disjoint reference. *Journal of Linguistic Research* 1.4.

Lebeaux, D. (1983). Locality and anaphoric binding. To appear in *The Linguistic Review*.

Levin, J. (1983). Government relations and the structure of INFL. In *MIT Working Papers in Linguistics* 5. Department of Linguistics and Philosophy, Massachusetts Institute of Technology.

Lightfoot, D. (1977). On traces and conditions on rules. In P. Culicover, T. Wasow, and A. Akmajian, eds., *Formal Syntax*. New York: Academic Press.

May, R. (1977). *The Grammar of Quantification*. Doctoral dissertation, Massachusetts Institute of Technology.

Milner, J.-C. (1979). Le système de la négation en français et l'opacité du sujet. *Langue Française* 44.

Milner, J.-C. (1982). *Ordres et raisons de langue*. Paris: Le Seuil.

Milsark, G. (1974). *Existential Sentences in English*. Doctoral dissertation, Massachusetts Institute of Technology.

Milsark, G. (1977). Towards an explanation of certain peculiarities of the existential construction in English. *Linguistic Analysis* 3.1.

Obenauer, H.-G. (1976). *Etudes de syntaxe interrogative du français*. Tübingen: Niemeyer.

Pesetsky, D. (1982a). Complementizer-trace phenomena and the Nominative Island Condition. *The Linguistic Review* 1.3.

Pesetsky, D. (1982b). *Paths and Categories*. Doctoral dissertation, Massachusetts Institute of Technology.

Postal, P. (1977). Antipassive in French. *Linguisticae Investigationes* 1.1.

Pulleyblank, D. (1980). Some binding constructions in Yoruba. Ms., Massachusetts Institute of Technology.

Riemsdijk, H. van (1978). *A Case Study in Syntactic Markedness*. Dordrecht: Foris Publications.

Riemsdijk, H. van (1981). On adjacency in phonology and syntax. In *Proceedings of the Eleventh Annual Meeting of the North Eastern Linguistic Society*. University of Massachusetts, Amherst.

Riemsdijk, H. van, and E. Williams (1981). NP-structure. *The Linguistic Review* 1.2.

Rizzi, L. (1982a). *Issues in Italian Syntax*. Dordrecht: Foris Publications.

Rizzi, L. (1982b). On chain formation. Ms., Università della Calabria.

Rouveret, A. (1980). Sur la notion de proposition finie, gouvernement et inversion. *Langages* 60.

Rouveret, A., and J.-R. Vergnaud (1980) (SRS). Specifying reference to the subject: French causatives and conditions on representations. *Linguistic Inquiry* 11.1.

Ruwet, N. (1972). *Théorie syntaxique et syntaxe du français*. Paris: Le Seuil.

Safir, K. (1982). *Syntactic Chains and the Definiteness Effect*. Doctoral dissertation, Massachusetts Institute of Technology.

Simpson, J. (1982). The role of PRO in Case-agreement. Ms., Massachusetts Institute of Technology.

Sportiche, D. (1981). Bounding nodes in French. *The Linguistic Review* 1.2.

Sportiche, D. (1983). *Structural Invariance and Symmetry in Syntax*. Doctoral dissertation, Massachusetts Institute of Technology.

Steriade, D. (1980). On the derivation of genitival relatives in Romance. Ms., Massachusetts Institute of Technology.

Stowell, T. (1981). *Origins of Phrase Structure*. Doctoral dissertation, Massachusetts Institute of Technology. (To be published by The MIT Press, Cambridge, Mass.)

Taraldsen, K. T. (1980). On the NIC, vacuous application and the *that*-trace filter. Bloomington, Ind.: Indiana University Linguistics Club.

Taraldsen, K. T. (1981). The theoretical interpretation of a class of marked extractions. In A. Belletti, L. Brandi, and L. Rizzi, eds., *Theory of Markedness in Generative Grammar*. Pisa: Scuola Normale Superiore.

Torrego, E. (1984). On inversion in Spanish and some of its effects. *Linguistic Inquiry* 15.1.

Vergnaud, J.-R. (1974). *French Relative Clauses*. Doctoral dissertation, Massachusetts Institute of Technology.

Vergnaud, J.-R. (forthcoming). *Dépendence formelle et niveau de représentation en syntaxe*. Amsterdam: Benjamin.

Wasow, T. (1979). *Anaphors in Generative Grammar*. Ghent: E. Story-Scientia.

Wehrli, E. (1983). Remarks on cliticization in French causatives. In *MIT Working Papers in Linguistics* 5. Department of Linguistics and Philosophy, Massachusetts Institute of Technology.

Williams, E. (1974). *Rule Ordering in Syntax*. Doctoral dissertation, Massachusetts Institute of Technology.

Williams, E. (1980). Predication. *Linguistic Inquiry* 11.1.

Williams, E. (1981a). Argument structure and morphology. *The Linguistic Review* 1.1.

Williams, E. (1981b). French causative constructions. Ms., University of Massachusetts at Amherst.

Zubizarreta, M.-L. (1979). Extraction from NP and reformulation of Subjacency. Ms., Massachusetts Institute of Technology.

Zubizarreta, M.-L. (1982). *On the Relationship of the Lexicon to Syntax*. Doctoral dissertation, Massachusetts Institute of Technology.

Index